Market Opportunity Analysis
Text and Cases

BEST BUSINESS BOOKS®
Robert E. Stevens, PhD
David L. Loudon, PhD
Editors in Chief

Doing Business in Mexico: A Practical Guide by Gus Gordon and Thurmon Williams

Employee Assistance Programs in Mananged Care by Norman Winegar

Marketing Your Business: A Guide to Developing a Strategic Marketing Plan by Ronald A. Nykiel

Customer Advisory Boards: A Strategic Tool for Customer Relationship Building by Tony Carter

Fundamentals of Business Marketing Research by David A. Reid and Richard E. Plank

Marketing Management: Text and Cases by David L. Loudon, Robert E. Stevens, and Bruce Wrenn

Selling in the New World of Business by Bob Kimball and Jerold "Buck" Hall

Many Thin Companies: The Change in Customer Dealings and Managers Since September 11, 2001 by Tony Carter

The Book on Management by Bob Kimball

The Concise Encyclopedia of Advertising by Kenneth E. Clow and Donald Baack

Application Service Providers in Business by Luisa Focacci, Robert J. Mockler, and Marc E. Gartenfeld

The Concise Handbook of Management: A Practitioner's Approach by Jonathan T. Scott

The Marketing Research Guide, Second Edition by Robert E. Stevens, Bruce Wrenn, Philip K. Sherwood, and Morris E. Ruddick

Marketing Planning Guide, Third Edition by Robert E. Stevens, David L. Loudon, Bruce Wrenn, and Phylis Mansfield

Concise Encyclopedia of Church and Religious Organization Marketing by Robert E. Stevens, David L. Loudon, Bruce Wrenn, and Henry Cole

The Economies of Competition: The Race to Monopoly by George G. Djolov

Market Opportunity Analysis: Text and Cases by Robert E. Stevens, Philip K. Sherwood, J. Paul Dunn, and David L. Loudon

Concise Encyclopedia of Real Estate Business Terms by Bill Roark and Ryan Roark

Concise Encyclopedia of Investing by Darren W. Oglesby

Marketing Research: Text and Cases, Second Edition by Bruce Wrenn, Robert Stevens, and David Loudon

Market Opportunity Analysis
Analysis
Text and Cases

Robert E. Stevens
Philip K. Sherwood
J. Paul Dunn
David L. Loudon

Routledge
Taylor & Francis Group

NEW YORK AND LONDON

Published by

Best Business Books®, an imprint of The Haworth Press, Inc., 10 Alice Street, Binghamton, NY 13904-1580.

Transferred to Digital Printing 2010 by Routledge
270 Madison Ave, New York NY 10016
2 Park Square, Milton Park, Abingdon, Oxon, OX14 4RN

The first edition of this book, *Market Analysis: Assessing Your Business Opportunities* (The Haworth Press, 1993), was authored by Robert E. Stevens, Philip K. Sherwood, and Paul Dunn.

PUBLISHER'S NOTE
The development, preparation, and publication of this work has been undertaken with great care. However, the Publisher, employees, editors, and agents of The Haworth Press are not responsible for any errors contained herein or for consequences that may ensue from use of materials or information contained in this work. The Haworth Press is committed to the dissemination of ideas and information according to the highest standards of intellectual freedom and the free exchange of ideas. Statements made and opinions expressed in this publication do not necessarily reflect the views of the Publisher, Directors, management, or staff of The Haworth Press, Inc., or an endorsement by them.

Cover design by Jennifer M. Gaska.

Library of Congress Cataloging-in-Publication Data

Market opportunity analysis : text and cases / Robert E. Stevens . . . [et al.].
    p. cm.
  Includes bibliographical references and index.
  ISBN-13: 978-0-7890-2418-3 (hc. : alk. paper)
  ISBN-10: 0-7890-2418-7 (hc. : alk. paper)
  ISBN-13: 978-0-7890-2419-0 (pbk. : alk. paper)
  ISBN-10: 0-7890-2419-5 (pbk. : alk. paper)
  1. Marketing research. 2. Consumer behavior. I. Stevens, Robert E., 1942-.

HF5415.2.M35545 2006
658.8'3—dc22

2005015271

CONTENTS

PART IV: INTERNAL ANALYSIS

CASES

ABOUT THE AUTHORS

Robert Stevens, PhD, is the John Massey Professor of Business at Southeastern Oklahoma State University in Durant, Oklahoma. He received his PhD from the University of Arkansas in 1971. During his distinguished career, Dr. Stevens has taught at the University of Arkansas, the University of Southern Mississippi, Oral Roberts University, University of Louisiana Monroe, and Hong Kong Shue Yan College. His repertoire of courses has included marketing management, marketing research, sales management, and strategic management. The author and co-author of 25 books and well over 150 other publications, he has published his research findings in a number of business journals and numerous professional conference proceedings. Dr. Stevens is a past co-editor of the *Journal of Ministry Marketing & Management* and currently co-editor of Haworth's *Services Marketing Quarterly,* and serves on the editorial boards of four other professional journals. He is also co-editor of Haworth's Best Business Books series. Dr. Stevens has acted as a marketing consultant to local, regional, and national organizations and is the owner of two small businesses.

Philip K. Sherwood, EdD, is Director of Research Services for Maritz Research. He has worked on both the supplier and client side of market research for more than 20 years, including 14 years with Maritz. Previously, he directed the primary and secondary research programs for the data storage division of the 3M and Imation Corporations. Dr. Sherwood has co-authored six books in the areas of market research, feasibility analysis, market opportunity analysis, and product development, including the *Marketing Research Guide, Second Edition* (Haworth) and *Market Analysis: Assessing Your Business Opportunities* (Haworth).

Paul Dunn, PhD, is Distinguished Professor of Entrepreneurship and Small Business, and Director of the Entrepreneurship Studies, the Small Business Institute, and the Small Business Development Center at The University of Louisiana at Monroe. He teaches entrepreneurship, new venture creation, and venture management at the graduate and undergraduate levels. Dr. Dunn has published more than

100 proceedings articles and journal articles, and is co-author of *Market Analysis: Assessing Your Business Opportunities* (Haworth).

David Loudon, PhD, is Professor of Marketing in the School of Business at Samford University. Dr. Loudon has taught a variety of courses but focuses on marketing management and services marketing. He has co-authored over a dozen books, including *Marketing Management: Text and Cases* (Haworth), and has written more than 100 papers, articles, and business cases. Dr. Loudon is the co-author of 12 books, including the *Marketing Planning Guide, Third Edition* (Haworth), and has conducted research in the United States, Europe, Asia, and Latin America on such topics as consumer behavior, international marketing, services marketing, and marketing management. He has written more 100 papers, articles, and business cases, and his research findings have been published in a number of journals and in the proceedings of numerous professional conferences. Dr. Loudon is co-editor of Best Business Books, an imprint of The Haworth Press, Inc., co-editor of *Services Marketing Quarterly* (Haworth), and past co-editor of the *Journal of Ministry Marketing & Management.*

Preface

Market Opportunity Analysis presents a systematic approach to feasibility analysis that is philosophically sound and practically oriented. The philosophical base is the strategic management orientation that is the cornerstone to the marketing process. The practical orientation is achieved through emphasis on techniques and tools used in preparing a feasibility analysis. A step-by-step approach is presented which carries the reader through the feasibility analysis process with the emphasis on what needs to be done and how to do it. The cases that accompany the text demonstrate the application of the techniques discussed in the book and provide an excellent tool to help students analyze and present solutions to actual situations involving market analysis.

There were three main reasons for writing this book. The first was out of a need as teachers and consultants for a book that covered feasibility analysis from a strategic viewpoint, yet in a practical, "How to do it" approach rather than a traditional academic orientation. In other words, we wanted our students to be able to conduct a feasibility analysis rather than just understand the process or discuss how it should be done.

The second reason grows out of the first. Since we were unable to find such a book, we developed our own approaches and put together a systematic format for conducting a feasibility analysis. Over the years, we have examined every book we could find on the topic for relevant material, tools, insights, and shortcomings, and then we put together a book which incorporated the good ideas but overcame the shortcomings.

The third reason for writing the book was that one of the most common types of decisions businesspeople make is whether or not to create a new business or introduce a new product. An extensive feasibility analysis is a prerequisite to such decisions. Thus, this book addresses a topic that most businesspeople are involved in and which produces significant "bottom-line" results.

PART I:
INTRODUCTION TO ASSESSING
BUSINESS OPPORTUNITIES

Chapter 1

Assessing Business Opportunities: An Overview

THE IMPORTANCE OF OPPORTUNITY ANALYSIS

The twenty-first century has ushered in an era of business that is perhaps one of the most challenging in history. Markets for many products have weakened; major firms face some of their most critical financial crises; international competition for major product categories is at an all-time high; and financial markets are in an upheaval due to interest rate changes, uncertainty over future rates, and shifting government policies on tax decreases, increases, and deficit spending. These are only some of the most obvious environmental factors business managers must cope with.

Although these changes have wreaked havoc in many industries, they have also caused many managers to reevaluate the basis of success in their own industries, and in business in general. Many realized that the key to success is planning—not just on a short-term basis, but on a time scale that is long-run or strategic in orientation.

This book concentrates on opportunity analysis, which is an intricate part of the strategic planning process. It covers not only how opportunity analysis relates to strategic planning, but also presents the techniques that can be used to carry out opportunity analysis. Thus, it is oriented toward building analytical skills for an individual manager by describing what should be done and how to do it.

FACTORS INFLUENCING FEASIBILITY ANALYSIS

The strategic alternatives of an enterprise are influenced by a number of factors. The factors are of three types: external, financial, and internal. External factors include market size, competition, technology, inflation and the economy, government regulations, political conditions, social change, and nature.

External Considerations

Market size. The size and makeup of markets for goods and services influence the nature of the opportunities an organization faces. The growth and longevity of markets influence not only whether opportunities will be pursued but also the level of commitment a firm will make to pursue an opportunity.

Competition. Some companies and some markets focus corporate strategy and strategic planning around the behavior or anticipated behavior of their competitors.

Technology. Major technological advances create opportunities for companies prepared to capitalize on them. The computer chip, electronic transistor, and synthetic fibers have all led to minor revolutions in their respective markets.

Inflation and the economy. After several decades of stable prices, inflation became a definite factor for planners in the 1970s. The basic economic conditions of a nation will determine the range of opportunities available to organizations. Conditions such as inflation, money supply, interest rates, and cash flow problems are part of the economic circumstances that confront firms today and require appropriate strategic planning. Even the largest and most powerful corporations encounter problems.

Government regulations. The role of government has increased in the regulation of economic life in all major industrial nations. It influences many phases of marketing, including distribution, advertising, price policy, product design, and consumer use. Although government regulations present both restraints and opportunities, their side effects have often been higher costs. Pollution control devices, reporting requirements, tax policy (windfall tax), safety policy, and other government controls and regulations have added costs to the industry and the consumer. Evaluation of past and proposed legislation is an essential part of strategic planning for all organizations.

Political conditions. The introduction of political risk should be an essential part of any organization's strategic planning. The oil crisis of 1974 and general political instability have altered the state of the art of planning within many companies depending upon unstable supplies of raw materials. A part of the international business environment that is unavoidable today is the potential uncertainty of political events. The overthrow of Saddam Hussein in Iraq; the continuing conflict in Northern Ireland; some fifteen to twenty wars, border clashes, and guerilla conflicts in Africa; and many other problems in various parts of the world have increased anxiety regarding the role of political risk in overseas investment. Strategic planners frequently use the word "turbulent" to describe the environment within which today's multinational companies must operate.

Social change. Social change presents opportunities as well as hazards to business enterprises. These influences change rather slowly over time; however, they can ultimately have a severe impact on the economic viability of a company. Social change can have a radical impact on the behavior of important groups of consumers. For example, technological innovation must be assimilated by the consumer in order to become economically viable. Although the technology is available for a checkless economic environment, society has not completely embraced it. Major research efforts are constantly tracking social changes and attempting to evaluate their impact on business. Since many important social changes move at a slow pace, businesses often fail to identify the significance of the change to their activities until it is too late to mitigate the damage or capitalize on the opportunity.

Nature. Droughts, floods, blizzards, earthquakes, hurricanes, and other natural events can all have important impact on business. In many cases, the capricious acts of nature are unpredictable but they represent environmental factors that require proper scenario planning.

Financial Considerations

Financial considerations reflect the financial impact of alternatives in terms of revenue estimates, cost estimates, and return on investment (ROI). They must reflect both the size of the investment needed to effectively compete in a market and the potential returns associated with that investment.

Revenue estimates. Revenue estimates provide the essential data needed to assess the impact of market entry by a new competitor. If a firm is considering entering an existing market it must assess its chances of attaining a given market share and thus a specific stream of revenues. The estimate of sales revenues along with cost estimates provide the essential data for pro forma analysis of an opportunity.

Cost estimates. Cost estimates reflect the level of costs that will be associated with the revenues generated by a proposed venture. All costs should be estimated to accurately reflect the income or cash flows that will be produced by an opportunity.

Return on investment (ROI). Given the estimates of future revenues and costs, the next step in financial analysis is the analysis of return on investment. Two concerns are present here: (1) the level of investment needed to compete effectively, and (2) the profitability potentials available given the investment level. In other words, "How much money will it take to pursue an alternative?" and "What type of earning can be produced?"

Internal Considerations

Internal considerations include: (1) purpose, (2) corporate objectives, and (3) resources.

Purpose. A statement of purpose or mission is management's expression of the nature of the organization. It answers the following questions: "What kind of organization are we?" and "What kind of organization do we want to be?" The definition of purpose or mission becomes the guiding force in strategic decisions because what we do should be a function of what we are.

Corporate objectives. A mission statement proposes to answer the question of what we are, and corporate objectives answer the question: "What do we want to accomplish?" Objectives become the specific ways a firm accomplished its organizational mission. These objectives also become the standard by which organizational effectiveness is judged. Effectiveness is measured by the firm's success in accomplishing its stated objectives.

Resources. The resources of an organization are the enabling factors that allow a firm to accomplish objectives. Resources are composed of the people, money, machinery, facilities, etc. a company either possesses or has the ability to acquire. Its people base and material asset base represent an organization's capabilities for pursuing opportunities.

Thus, external factors define the nature of the opportunity, the financial considerations tell us the financial impact of the opportunity, and the internal factors determine whether a firm should pursue an opportunity (mission and objectives) and whether it is capable (resources) of pursuing an opportunity.

WHAT IS OPPORTUNITY ANALYSIS?

Opportunity analysis is the process of defining the exact nature of the opportunities available in an organization's operating environment in terms of external, financial, and internal considerations. Figure 1.1 presents an overview of this process in terms of the steps involved in the analysis.

As this diagram depicts, opportunity analysis is a comprehensive analysis of all aspects of an alternative before decisions are made to pursue it. The results of such an analysis put the decision maker in a position of having a strong data base from which to choose among the various alternatives present in the environment in line with financial and internal considerations that are specified by management.

The analysis begins with a detailed study of the environment in which the proposed business would operate. This includes not only the legal, political, economic, social, cultural, and technological environment but also market size, growth trends, and consumers' attitudes and behavior. It also involves a study of current and potential competitors who may be going after the same customers you propose to attract. These factors are external to the organization or person contemplating the new venture and therefore a great deal of diligence is required for a thorough analysis of these factors. This usually involves a substantial commitment of time and money to collect the information used in the analysis.

If this analysis indicates that these factors are favorable to the potential business, then an analysis of the financial implications of the opportunity should be undertaken. The financial analysis is the key to determining the potential profitability of the business and the expected ROI. The results of this analysis provide the information which can be used to attract investors and/or lenders who may be approached to obtain capital for the venture.

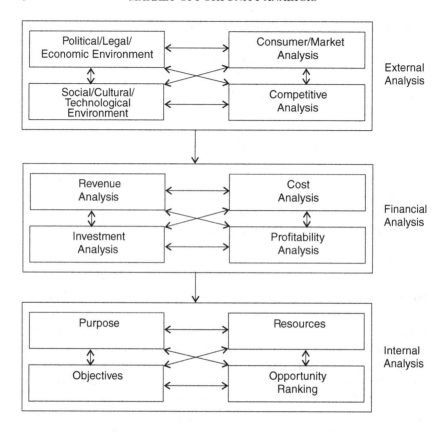

FIGURE 1.1. The opportunity assessment process.

The final area of analysis involves a study of internal factors which affect the decision to pursue a given opportunity. The organization's or individual's purpose, objectives, and resources must be analyzed in relation to the proposed opportunity. An opportunity, even a potentially profitable one, may not "fit" with the purpose, the objectives, or the resources of the organization. Such opportunities are forgone for others that do "fit."

As Figure 1.1 emphasizes, a thorough study of the opportunity is completed *before* a decision is made to pursue it. Rushing into a decision without the type of analysis described in this book greatly magnifies increases the chances of failure. Although failures cannot be completely eliminated because of unforeseen circumstances, the chance of success can be greatly enhanced by thoroughly assessing the opportunities before commitments are made. A 1990 article dealing with factors that lead to failure listed "guessing instead of digging" as the number one way to scuttle a new business.[1]

PLAN OF THE BOOK

Part I presents the foundation for opportunity analysis, which is strategic planning. Chapters 1 and 2 provide the framework from which opportunity analysis can be viewed as an integral part of the strategic management process.

Part II contains two chapters that deal with external analysis. Environmental factors, market size and growth, and competitive analysis are given detailed treatment.

Part III covers financial analysis. The procedures used to estimate revenues, costs, and ROI are presented to provide complete coverage of this vital area.

Part IV presents internal analysis. It contains the material that moves from analysis to decision making as internal factors are evaluated in light of the alternatives being considered. This material synthesizes all the analysis in a form that summarizes the analysis in one worksheet as the basis for selecting alternatives. It includes an outline of a business plan as well as sources of funds for new business opportunities.

In order to apply the concepts addressed in the book, ten cases are supplied. These cover a variety of organization size and type, and will be useful in further understanding the nature of market opportunity analysis.

Chapter 2

Strategic Management and Planning

Many of today's most successful companies evolved out of an era when they introduced a good product or service onto a market that was ready to accept it. Growth was achieved by expanding to new geographical markets and later by adding new products to build a complete line of products rather than concentrating on any one in particular. In many companies, growth just appeared to happen with little or no formal thought about the management processes that were bringing forth the growth in company operations.

However, with significant shifts in economic, environmental, and competitive forces, most managers have now realized that for survival and growth to occur they must be much more aware of the impact of the decisions they are making and the management processes used to make these decisions. A switch to strategic planning is replacing the more intuitive decision-making approaches used in prior years. The key to success for most companies is strategic planning and the key to strategic planning rests on the matching of market needs to corporate capabilities—"strategic fit."[1]

WHY STRATEGIC PLANNING?

Out of a large number of decisions made by an organization's managers there are a handful of critical ones that can significantly impact the future of that organization. These strategic decisions require identification and thoughtful consideration. In the past several decades, many major American corporations have focused on short-term results relative to market position and profitability. In the meantime the Japanese have made great strides because of their very specific strategic planning approach. They have been willing to sacrifice short-term profitability for market share.

Perspectives of strategic thinking can be illustrated with this question: *Who are the two most important persons responsible for the success of an airplane's flight?* Frequent responses are:

- The pilot and the navigator
- The pilot and the maintenance supervisor
- The pilot and the air traffic controller
- The pilot and the flight engineer

All of these responses recognize the day-to-day hands-on importance of the pilot. They all introduce one of several other important support or auxiliary functionaries to the answer. However, each of these segmented responses ignores the one person who is perhaps the single most important individual to the ultimate success of the airplane—the designer. Perhaps the pilot and the designer are the two most important individuals to the success of an airplane. The pilot because of his or her day-to-day responsibilities in commanding the craft and the designer because of his or her ability to create a concept that can be economically constructed, easily operated by any normally competent flight crew, and maintained safely by the ground crew. Most modern executives perceive themselves as the "pilot" of the organization; taking off, landing, conferring with the navigator, and communicating with the air traffic controller. They generally view themselves as chief, hands-on operational managers. However, what has been most lacking in American industry in the past few years has been an appreciation for the long-run strategic viewpoint. More emphasis needs to be placed on the "designer" approach to operating an organization. A well-conceived strategic planning system can facilitate this emphasis.

STRATEGIC PLANNING: KEY TO SUCCESS

Many of the large business combinations of the 1920s did not survive into the 1950s. And those that were successful in the 1960s were sometimes faltering by the end of the century. For example, there has been trouble in the auto industry and difficulty with some large equipment manufacturers and some financial institutions. Strategic planning is helpful for companies to anticipate and avoid problems. But strategic planning development must not lead to simply a larger number of people creating reports for people to read. It cannot become an appendage activity that has little direct impact on the actual making of goods and services. Strategic planning is consistent with decreasing overhead and increasing productivity. In fact, the lack of strategic orientation is considered by many as the biggest problem facing industry today. In order to successfully compete, a company must strategically eliminate the high overhead structure that is characteristic of the end of an economic long wave.

Planning is one of the keys to success of any undertaking and nowhere is it more important than in business. Every study of business failures uncovers the same basic problem, whether it is called undercapitalization, poor location, or simply a lack of managerial skills. All of these problems have their roots in poor planning. Strategic planning of operations from a market perspective can become a key to long-term survival and growth of an organization.

WHAT IS STRATEGY?

Before discussing the market opportunity analysis process in more detail, clear-cut definitions of the terms *strategic* and *strategy* need to be established. This will provide a better perspective of market opportunity analysis because it is an integral part of the process of strategy development.

"Strategy" is derived from the Greek word which means generalship, art of the general, or more broadly, leadership. The word strategic when used in the context of planning provides a perspective to planning which is long-run in nature and deals with achieving specified end results. Just as military strategy has as its objective the winning of the war, so too, strategic planning has as its objective achievement of corporate objectives—survival and growth.

Strategic decisions must be differentiated from tactical decisions. Strategic decisions outline the overall game plan or approach, while tactical decisions involve implementing the various activities which are needed to carry out a strategy.

Polo, by Ralph Lauren, was positioned as an upscale brand of clothing aimed at the male market. This was a strategic decision made by executives for this product line. Given this strategy, many tactical decisions were made about the styles and prices of the clothing, the atmosphere in which the clothes were worn in advertising, the image portrayed by the people used in the ads, and the quality of stores distributing Polo clothes. These were tactical decisions that needed to carry out or implement the strategic decisions previously made. Thus, the strategic decision provides the overall framework within which the tactical decisions are made. Managers must be able to differentiate between these types of decisions to identify whether the decision has short-term or long-term implications.

RESISTANCE TO STRATEGIC PLANNING

Although there is much academic and theoretical support for strategic planning, the actual implementation of it often runs aground on the shores of corporate reality. Even among high-tech companies you find significant resistance to strategic planning. Some of the most common arguments against strategic planning are:

1. Planning is not action-oriented.
2. Planning takes too much time; we are too busy to plan.
3. Planning is unrealistic because of the rapid change in our industry (technological uncertainty, etc).
4. Planning becomes an end, not just a means to an end.

Many of these arguments stem from the same kind of thinking that would feel that the pilot was the most important person in the success of an airplane referring back to the airplane/designer analogy. To be helpful, strategic planning does not depend on complete forecasting accuracy. In fact, a variety of futuristic alternatives or scenarios can be very useful in establishing strategic planning parameters. Often a best-case, most-likely case, and worst-case approach is used. This three-level forecast gives dimension to the process of recognizing, anticipating, and "managing" change.

The feeling that strategic planning is not "hands-on" and related to the important day-to-day operations of the company is a frequent view found in American industry. However, this point of view is short-sighted in terms of long-term success and profitability. Strategic planning is not just for dreamers, in fact, it lets the management team determine what can be done today to accomplish or avoid some future circumstance.

Strategic planning can become an end in the minds of some practitioners. This is particularly true when established solely as a staff responsibility within an organization. A support staff can facilitate the strategic planning process, but the process will not be a dynamic lifeblood activity of the organization without the ongoing involvement of top management and line managers. President Eisenhower has been widely quoted as saying, "Plans are nothing, planning is everything." The trust he expressed was that the actual plan itself was not the end itself, but that the process of planning—developing futuristic scenarios, evaluating the environment and competition, assessing internal strengths and capabilities, revising objectives and tactics—was the organization dialogue that was most important. This organizational dialogue ideally breaks down barriers of communication, exposes blind spots to the light, tests logic, measures the environment, and determines feasibility. The end result is more effective and efficient implementation of organizational activity.

THE STRATEGIC MANAGEMENT PROCESS

The strategic management process, whether done at a corporate level involving whole companies or divisions or at an individual product/service level involving a single product or service, is basically a matching process. This matching process involves analyzing opportunities in the marketplace as a market develops and then matching company resources to opportunities. The objective of this process is to peer through the "strategic window"[2] and identify opportunities that exist in the market for which the individual company is equipped to take advantage of or respond to. Thus the *strategic management process can be defined as a managerial process which involves matching organizational capabilities to market opportunities*. These opportunities are created as a market evolves over time and decisions revolve around investing or divesting resources in these markets. The context in which these strategic decisions are made is: (1) the organization's operating environment, (2) company purpose or mission, and (3) objectives. This overall process is depicted in Figure 2.1. Market opportunity analysis is the process that ties all these elements together to facilitate strategic choices that are consistent with all three areas.

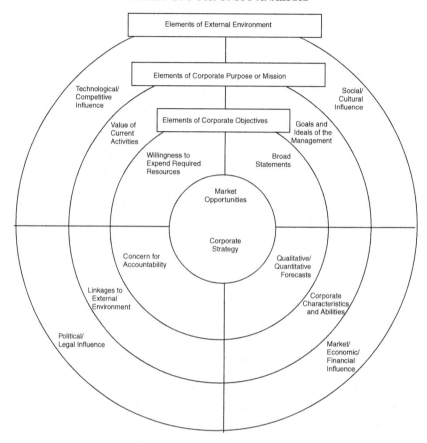

FIGURE 2.1. The strategic management process.

A prerequisite to effective strategic planning is identifying the unit or level for that planning is to be done. Many companies have embraced a concept that is extremely useful in this strategic planning process—the strategic business unit.

A strategic business unit (SBU) meets the following criteria:

1. It has a clearly defined market.
2. It faces identifiable competitors in an external market (as opposed to being an internal supplier).

3. As a separate, distinct, and identifiable unit whose assets do not depend on the existence of another SBU, its manager has control over planning and decision areas that determine success of the business.[3]

Once an organization's SBUs are identified, the strategic planning can be carried out for each SBU. However, care must be exercised to insure that the activities of each SBU are interrelated to the corporate level objectives and purpose.

CORPORATE PURPOSE OR MISSION

Peter Drucker refers to an organization's purpose as its mission or reason for being.[4] To define a business's purpose is to ask,

> What is our business and more importantly, what should it be. Only a clear definition of the mission and purpose of the business make possible clear and realistic business objectives. It is the foundation for priorities, strategies, plans, and work assignments. It is the starting point for the design of managerial jobs and, above all, for the design of managerial structure.[5]

One aspect of every firm's purpose should be to meet a need in the marketplace. However, a statement of purpose needs to be a written statement which spells out in some detail the uniqueness that has led to the creation of the business enterprise. Such a statement becomes a reference point for subsequent managerial action. In effect, it becomes the reference point on which all operating areas in a firm must reflect as a part of their decision making processes. A typical type of question faced by most firms is: "Do we enter a particular market or introduce a particular product?" The starting point in answering should be how this decision relates to accomplishing the stated purpose of the organization. If it does not help the organization accomplish its stated purpose, it should not be undertaken, no matter how profitable or otherwise successful it appears to be; it is not aligned with the basic purpose of the enterprise. A firm's purpose can be altered over time to reflect changing environmental conditions or changing managerial philosophies, but at any given point there must be a standard of relevance for managerial thought and action.

A clear understanding of company purpose is needed to insure alignment of activities with the way the firm has defined its mission. Otherwise attempted activities will be at cross-purposes with the organizational mission, or on the other hand, there will be a failure to attempt activities beneficial to fulfillment of its purpose. *Common vision and unity can be achieved only by common purpose.*

The following statement of purpose was prepared by Colowyo Coal Company's management and is exemplary of the type of statement that can be developed to provide unity and guidance in decision making.

> The primary purpose of Colowyo Coal Company is to operate at a profit for the benefit of its owners, employees, and the community. Colowyo will produce its coal resources at optimum rates that will provide orderly community growth, protect the environment and contribute to alleviating our nation's energy needs.
>
> The Company is committed to adhering to its approved mining plan by following all laws, rules, and applications with a minimum disturbance to the environment and timely restoration to disturbed areas.
>
> Our purpose is to produce a quality product and to provide superior services to its customers. Colowyo will provide a work environment for its employees that allows them, through training and other means, to achieve personal growth while helping the Company to achieve its stated objectives.
>
> An equal opportunity employer, Colowyo makes every effort to provide safe, healthful working conditions for its employees as it seeks to operate within the tenants of the free enterprise system.
>
> Finally, Colowyo is committed to conducting its business relationships in such a manner as to be a credit to its partners, employees, and their families, customers and the community. The Company is proud to be a leader in the mining industry for our country.[6]

A few of the implications of this statement for market opportunity analysis will help show how to relate a purpose to opportunity assessment.

The first paragraph, for example, states that the company will produce at an optimum rate that provides orderly community growth, protects the environment, and so on. This means that the strategies must not be based on an expansion of sales volume, which would cause a large increase in productive capacity and would involve both rapid community growth and less environmentally compatible production techniques.

Another restraint can be derived from the third paragraph—"quality product." This stipulation limits market activities aimed at lower product quality to reach more cost-oriented customers or customers actually wanting a lower quality product.

These examples illustrate the impact of statements of purpose on opportunity analysis. Market activities must be consistent with overall purpose for an effective organization.

CORPORATE OBJECTIVES

Corporate objectives vary so widely in their nature, content, and specificity that it is difficult to describe a common "state of the art" of what corporate objectives should be. Even the terms used to describe objectives vary widely: policies, goals, values, and objectives, are often used interchangeably even within the same company. The definition used here is a generally accepted view of what is meant by objectives.

Basically, an objective is an end result desired, a statement of what is to be accomplished by an organization. The objective is tied to purpose in that achieving it is the way the organization fulfills its purpose.

Three objectives basic to any organization are to

1. Engage in a business activity that is both economically and socially useful.
2. Maintain and/or survive as a business entity.
3. Grow in size of operations—whether measured in sales, profits, number of employees, or some other growth criteria.

These objectives are almost inherent to a business even though many firms do not formally state them. However, to provide more

specific guidance to the organization as both a statement of end results sought and as a tool for evaluating performance, objectives need
to be more explicit in defining what is to be accomplished.

Peter Drucker points out the importance of objectives being more
than abstractions in the following statement: "If objectives are only
good intentions they are worthless. They must degenerate into work.
And work is always specific, always has—or should have—unam-
biguous measurable results, a deadline and a specific assignment of
accountability."[7]

Exhibit 2.1 shows some examples of corporate objectives taken
from statements of objectives of two corporations. Notice the differences in the degree of specificity of the objectives. Some companies
state their objectives in a more quantifiable format and others do not.
When objectives are quantified, they can be evaluated on an absolute
quantitative basis. Otherwise, they must be analyzed on the basis of
what was accomplished on a relative basis, relative to other years and
perhaps other companies.

CORPORATE STRATEGIES

The final stage in the strategic planning process is the development
of the overall corporate strategies that will be used to accomplish objectives.

Designing strategies is a process that involves: (1) identifying strategic options, (2) assessing options, and (3) selecting the strategy or
strategies. Before a strategy is selected, opportunities must be identified and defined. The rest of this chapter discusses a very useful approach to identifying opportunities. The definition of the exact nature
of opportunities is discussed in detail in Chapters 3 through 6.

Basic Growth Strategies

Since most companies have growth as one of their basic objectives,
one area of strategy development revolves around the question of how
growth will be obtained. Three possible alternative growth strategies are:

1. Product/market expansion strategies
2. Integrative strategies
3. Diversification strategies

EXHIBIT 2.1. Examples of corporate objectives.

Company 1

Financial Goals and Objectives

Management believes these standards are appropriate guides for development of plans and evaluation of performance over time. These goals include

- Earning the highest possible return on shareholders' equity consistent with responsible business practices;
- Ensuring repetitive, predictable, and steadily growing per-share profits and dividends as the yield from an ample stream of reinvestments; and
- Performing consistently better than the industry in every market where the company's products and services compete.

These goals translate into the following financial objectives:

- Annual earnings per-share growth of 12 to 15 percent.
- Pretax return on average invested capital of 25 percent.
- After-tax return on average stockholders' equity of 18 percent.
- A strong "A" credit rating on senior debt of the parent company.

Company 2

Customer Service and Product Quality

To supply gas and electric service for the home, the community, commerce, agriculture, industry, and government:

- At the lowest possible cost
- In the quantities customers demand
- With constantly improved quality
- With increasing beneficial uses of our service

Profitability

To earn an adequate profit so that:

- Investors' risk and replacement and obsolescence of capital assets can be provided for
- Earnings can be reinvested and new capital can be attracted and retained
- The company's total efforts and net effectiveness will be financially sound

These strategic alternatives can be illustrated in a 2 × 2 matrix called a product/market growth matrix. This type of matrix is illustrated in Figure 2.2.

Product/Market Expansion Strategies

Product/market expansion strategies involve growth through expansion of existing product markets, development of new products aimed at existing markets, or development of new markets for existing products. Each of these strategic options carries with it advantages and risks as far as management is concerned. In a market penetration strategy, management has the advantage of both product knowledge and existing markets. The obvious disadvantage is the fact that the products will eventually pass through various product life-cycle stages ending with sales decline and extinction.

In a product development strategy, the advantage management has is in knowledge of the market they are dealing with since the products are aimed at existing markets. The disadvantage is lack of product knowledge.

When a market development strategy is used, product knowledge is the advantage, and market knowledge is the disadvantage. When a diversification strategy is used, management is under the most strain. They have neither product knowledge nor market knowledge as an advantage so they must quickly acquire this knowledge or rely on acquiring managers or companies who already possess product/ market knowledge.

	EXISTING PRODUCTS	NEW PRODUCTS
EXISTING MARKETS	1. MARKET PENETRATION	2. PRODUCT DEVELOPMENT
NEW MARKETS	3. MARKET DEVELOPMENT	4. DIVERSIFICATION

FIGURE 2.2. Product/market growth matrix.

Market penetration involves growth by increasing sales of existing products in existing markets. This expansion of sales can come about by: (1) altering purchase patterns of existing customers—getting them to buy more when they purchase or to purchase more frequently; (2) attracting nonusers to purchase the product; and (3) attracting purchasers of competitors' products to switch, thereby increasing market share. Alternatives 1 and 2 involve increasing the total size of the market, and alternative 3 involves increasing market share.

Product development is increasing sales through the introduction of new products to existing markets. Product development involves altering existing products by: (1) adding new features, (2) offering different quality levels, or (3) offering different sizes of the product.

Market development entails offering existing products to new markets. These markets can be: (1) new geographical markets such as foreign countries, or (2) new market segments not currently using the product.

Integrative Strategies

A company can choose as a strategic alternative growth through integration of activities within its current industry. Three alternatives for this type of growth are: (1) forward integration, (2) backward integration, and (3) horizontal integration.

Forward integration means the company looks "down" the channel of distribution to the next channel members who currently represent a customer type. For example, a manufacturer who "looks down the channel" sees either wholesalers or retailers as the next channel member. Thus, forward integration takes the form of expanding—either internally or through acquisitions—through taking over wholesaling or retailing functions.

Backward integration seeks growth through ownership of companies "up the channel," in other words, suppliers of products or raw materials. A manufacturer of automotive tires who builds its own plant to product synthetic fibers used in tire production would be growing through backward integration.

Horizontal integration seeks growth through ownership of competitors. This strategy involves identifying and acquiring firms which are in competition with the firm seeking growth.

Diversification Strategies

A final strategic alternative for growth is through diversification. Diversification entails introducing new products into new markets or acquiring other firms that are already in these new product/market situations. Diversification strategies can take various forms. The most common are: (1) product/technology-related, (2) market-related, and (3) non–product/non–market-related.

Product/technology-related diversification consists of adding products which are technologically related to existing products even though they are aimed at different markets. A company that manufactures electronic watches for the consumer market developing a line of industrial gauges using the same electronic technology would be an example of this type of diversification.

Market-related diversification consists of introducing products aimed at the same market even though the product technologies are different. A company that manufactures and markets a line of cosmetics, for example, could introduce a cosmetic bag. This product would be aimed at the same market as cosmetics but involves quite different product technologies.

Non–product/Non–market-related diversification, sometimes called conglomerate diversification, seeks to add new products aimed at new classes of customers. The family-oriented entertainment company referred to earlier offers an example of this type of diversification. They introduced a new water-related recreation park aimed at the nontourist market whereas their prior business efforts had been concentrated on non–water-related entertainment appealing to the tourist market.

The growth strategies previously described provide alternatives for a company seeking growth. Although each type was treated as a separate strategic alternative, more than one strategy can be pursued at the same time, given the managerial and financial resources needed for such growth.

STRATEGIES FOR EXISTING SBUs

The Boston Consulting Group, a well-known consulting organization, has developed an approach to strategic planning that permits classifying SBUs on the basis of their relative market share and growth potential. This approach, depicted in Figure 2.3, permits development of strategies for each SBU based on its classification within the matrix. The vertical axis shows annualized market-growth rates for each SBU in its respective market. The division of high-low rates at 10 percent is arbitrary.

The horizontal axis shows the market share of each SBU in relation to the industry leaders. Thus it is relative market share and not absolute market share that is being measured. If relative market share for an SBU is 1.5, this means that SBU is the market leader and its share

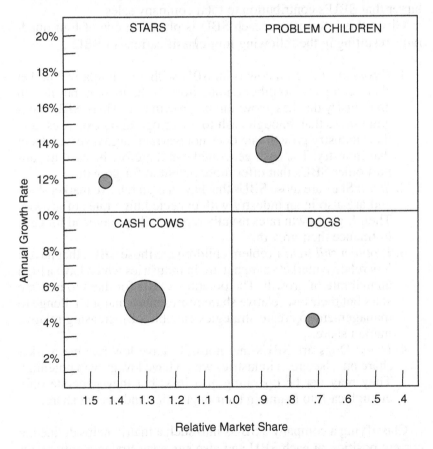

FIGURE 2.3. The Boston Consulting Group matrix. *Source:* Adapted from B. Hedley, "Strategy and the Business Portfolio," *Long Range Planning,* February 1977, p. 12.

is one-and-a-half times greater than the next closest competitor. A relative market share of .8 would indicate that the SBU's market share was 80 percent of the market leaders' share. Relative market shares put each SBU in relation to the leader and provide more information about market position than would absolute market share. The 1.5 × division is, again, an arbitrary point for separating SBUs into high-low relative market shares.

The size of the circle represents the proportional dollar contribution of each SBU to total company sales. The larger the circle, the larger that SBU's contribution to total company sales.

Given this information, each SBU is placed in one of four quadrants resulting in the following four classifications of SBUs.

1. *Cash cows:* A cash cow is an SBU with a high relative market share compared to other competitors in the market, but it is in an industry that has a low annual growth rate. These SBUs generate more than enough cash to cover operating expenses, and their industry growth rate does not warrant large investments in that industry. The cash generated can therefore be used to support other SBUs that offer more potential for growth.
2. *Stars:* Stars are those SBUs that have a high relative market share and are also in an industry with expected high rates of growth. Their high growth rates usually represent high demand for cash to finance their growth.
3. *Problem children:* Problem children are those SBUs that have a low relative market share but are in industries which have a high annual rate of growth. The potential exists for them to become stars but their low relative share represents a major challenge to management to create strategies capable of increasing relative market share.
4. *Dogs:* Dogs are SBUs that not only have low relative market share but also are in industries which have low growth potential. They may not be operating at a loss, but they generate only enough cash to maintain their operations and market share.

Classifying a company's SBUs into such a matrix helps define the current position of each SBU and also suggests strategic options for management to improve performance. Although the position of an SBU will change over time due to changes in growth rates or market position, the following four strategic actions are implied for the four cells: (1) "milk" cows, (2) "shine" stars, (3) "solve" problems, and (4) "shoot" dogs.

1. *"Milk" cows:* The strategy for cash cows is to spend enough on them to maintain their market share ("keep them healthy") so they can continue to generate cash.
2. *"Shine" stars:* The strategy for stars is to continue to invest funds into these SBUs to support their growth rate and high market shares. They will eventually slow in growth and become cash cows themselves and help generate funds for new stars.
3. *"Solve" problems:* The strategy for these SBUs would involve one of two options: (1) develop and test strategies for improving market share, or (2) divest of these SBUs and use the cash for supporting other more promising SBUs.
4. *"Shoot" dogs:* SBUs with low share, low growth potential are prime prospects for divestiture. Cash generated by divesting of these SBUs can be reinvested in other SBUs with more potential.

SUMMARY

This chapter provided an overview of the strategic planning process, which is the foundation for opportunity analysis. As management goes through the process of strategic planning, each strategic option must be viewed as an opportunity which must be carefully analyzed before a decision is made to select a given option. Thus, opportunity analysis is a prerequisite for successful strategic moves by a company.

The following chapters are designed to provide a detailed examination of the procedures and tools that can be used to complete opportunity analysis. Opportunity analysis begins with an analysis of market demand, which is the subject of the next two chapters.

PART II:
EXTERNAL ANALYSIS

Chapter 3

Market Demand Analysis

Analysis of market demand involves: (1) identifying a market, (2) identifying market factors, (3) estimating market potential, and (4) estimating the revenues anticipated from a given venture. This chapter examines three of the steps. The procedures for estimating revenues are discussed in Chapter 5, after the analysis of competition's impact on a given market is discussed in Chapter 4.

IDENTIFYING A MARKET

One fundamental concept underlying the type of analysis described in this chapter is that what is sometimes referred to as a market for a product or service is actually a composite of smaller markets, each with identifiable characteristics. When we speak of the automobile market, we are making reference to a large market which is composed of smaller submarkets or segments. This market can be segmented in several ways to identify the various submarkets. The size of the car different consumers want, for example, could be used to identify at least four submarkets or segments: full-size, intermediate, compact, and subcompacts. This process of breaking up a market into its constituent parts is called market segmentation. The basic premise is that the consumers in one market are different from the consumers in another, and therefore each represents a separate entity.

Markets are too complex and diverse to consider all consumers within the market as homogeneous. If a new product or service is to appeal to teenagers, for example, then that segment or part of the total market between the ages of thirteen and nineteen is the market of interest. Its size and characteristics must be identified and studied and not the other segments, which are not considered.

BASES FOR MARKET SEGMENTATION

Several commonly used bases for segmentation include: geographic, demographic, product usage, and product benefits. A discussion of the use of market grids is presented in this section to show how several of the bases can be combined for analysis and construction of individual market segments.

Geographic and Demographic Segmentation

The most commonly used basis for segmentation involves using geographic and demographic variables to segment markets. Geographic segmentation involves use of census tracts, cities, trade areas, counties, states, regions, and countries as the basis of segmentation. For many products, this is a logical framework. Snowmobiles, for example, are purchased in areas with sufficient snowfall. These areas can be geographically identified as one basis for segmentation.

Demographic segmentation involves using variables such as gender, age, income, educational level, etc., as the bases for segmenting a market. In the market grids used in the following section, age and gender are used as two variables to segment the clothing market. These variables are appropriate for many products and services.

Geographic and demographic characteristics of industrial consumers can also be useful in segmenting industrial markets. In fact, some customers are concentrated both geographically and by industry in certain industrial markets. Tire manufacturers in Ohio and electronics manufacturers in California are two examples.

Segmentation by Product Usage

A recent approach to market segmentation concentrates on the product usage patterns of consumers as the basis for segmentation. Consumers are classified as users or nonusers and users are further classified as light, medium, and heavy users. In most product categories, a small percentage of the consumers account for a majority of the purchases. Air travel, car rental, dog food, and hair coloring are such products. Thus usage rates become important as a basis for segmentation for some products.

Benefit Segmentation

Another way to segment markets is based on the benefits the buyers expect to receive upon purchase or use of a product. In one study, the toothpaste market was segmented on such bases as flavor and product appearance, brightness of teeth, decay prevention, and price. Each of these variables represents the principal benefits sought by the purchaser. Each of these benefit segments, in turn, is composed of consumers with different demographics, personalities, lifestyles, etc. Thus, each represents a distinct market segment.

MARKET GRIDS

One basic tool which can be used to segment a market is a market grid. A market grid is a two-dimensional view of a market which is divided into various segments using *characteristics* of *potential consumers*. Two important concepts in grid analysis are that *characteristics* of potential consumers are used to segment the market rather than product characteristics. This insures a market-oriented view of the market rather than a product-oriented view. Also characteristics of *potential* consumers rather than existing consumers are used to focus on consumers that the firm may not currently serve.

A series of grids must normally be used to completely describe a market so you must begin with a set of characteristics thought to be useful in differentiating consumers. Each characteristic must be analyzed to determine its probable effect on a market.

The characteristics normally include geographic, socioeconomic, behavioral, and/or psychological dimensions. The objective is to isolate a specific market rather than a general market. Most products or services are not consumed by just anyone so those people or companies which are most likely to consume an offering must be identified.

Once a list of potential consumer characteristics has been developed, the next step is actual grid construction. Figures 3.1 and 3.2 show two grids for shoes. Each section within the grid is actually a market segment for shoes. Notice that as each characteristic is used to identify a specific segment it becomes possible to begin to describe a market which, in turn, permits collecting data on a specific market.

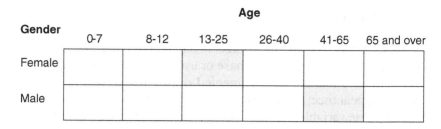

FIGURE 3.1. Grid One for shoes.

Income

Activity	Lower	Middle	Upper
Leisure			
Formal			
Work			
Recreation and Sport			

FIGURE 3.2. Grid Two for shoes.

These grids illustrate the breakdown approach to market segmentation where the total market is broken up into various submarkets.

The two shaded areas in the first grid represent two completely different market segments. The styles of shoes needed, the emphasis on styles, and the types of stores these consumers would prefer to shop at, buying motives—all of these would normally be quite different and represent different markets.

In the second grid, it also becomes apparent that the consumers represented by the two shaded areas (segments) represent different markets. You would not expect a sanitation worker and a bank president to need the same types of shoes for work; they may not shop at the same retail outlets, etc. As a market segment emerges through the analysis, it represents a potential group of consumers with similar characteristics that define a market. For smaller companies only one or a few segments may be of interest, whereas a large firm may develop or already have a complete line of products or services and therefore select several segments as potential target markets. Whether one or many segments are selected, this type of analysis is needed.

Some of the types of characteristics for consumer and industrial markets that may serve as a basis for segmentation are shown in Table 3.1.

Another approach to developing a grid or diagram to represent a market would be a *buildup approach.* This approach involves identifying the individual market segments and then putting the segments together to represent a market. The result is the same: a recognition of the differences in needs of different consumers.

An example of this approach for an industrial product is shown in Figure 3.3. This is a reconstruction of the market for component parts going into "downhole equipment" used on oil rigs. In conducting the

TABLE 3.1. Consumer characteristics by consumer type.

Type	Characteristic	Consumer
Socioeconomic	*Ultimate Consumers:*	*Industrial:*
	Age	Size—volume
	Gender	Number of employees
	Income	Number of plants
	Occupation	Type of organization
	Education	Industry
	Marital status	
Behavioral*	Brands purchased	Decision-making patterns
	Coupon redemption	Growth potential
	Store shopped	Public versus private
	Loyalty	Distribution pattern
Psychological*	Attitudes	Management attitudes
	Personality traits	Management awareness
	Awareness	Management style
	Recall	Management values
	Hobbies	
	Reading interest	

*These would include psychographic characteristics.

FIGURE 3.3. The buildup approach: OEM market for component parts—centrifugal pumps.

consumer analysis, it was found that the market was dominated by one firm. This firm accounted for about 80 percent of the original equipment market (OEM) sales in this market, with the rest of the sales volume going to several other firms. The large manufacturer was designated a key account, meaning it was considered as a distinct segment of the market. This approach still deals with complete segments, which are combined with other segments to form a market. Sometimes it is beneficial to move from individuals to segments to markets as discussed in the following text.

AN ALTERNATE APPROACH TO MARKET SEGMENTATION

Some entrepreneurs find it difficult to attempt to deal with the traditional approach to segmentation. This is true because one must be able to envision several dimensions of a particular segment at one time. That is, you think about the different income levels in a given population and then you attempt to envision how those in different age groups would be distributed among income groups and so on. To avoid such confusion, an alternative approach has been developed.

This alternative approach allows entrepreneurs to deal with the characteristics of each segment without having to deal with the various dimensions at one time. This approach is implemented by entrepreneurs visualizing the people they would expect to be in their market using very specific segmenting dimensions such as demographics, behavioral patterns, geographic location, and benefits. If entrepreneurs have an opportunity to visit a similar business, they might watch customers coming through the door and mentally record the relevant dimensions for segments in a general way.

Segments should be internally homogeneous and externally heterogeneous with respect to the relevant segmenting dimensions. That is, if age is a relevant dimension, the customers in one segment should be similar in age and those in other segments should be quite different ages from those in other segments.

The basic approach is to identify one customer to serve as the "core element" for a segment. Once that has been done, the entrepreneur sits down with that person and identifies the value or nature of each relevant segmenting characteristic (i.e., age, gender, benefits, geographic location, etc.). Once all the relevant dimensions are identified, the entrepreneur aggregates all the other people with those characteristics around the "core element." The core element's name may be assigned to the segment to give the entrepreneur a clear point of reference. A clearly identifiable segment has been created.

The next step is to pick another core element quite different from the first and go through the same process until the second segment is created. The process can be continued until all clearly identifiable segments have been identified. A final step might be to eliminate any common segment characteristics in all segments to further refine the definition of each segment.

After segments have been identified, the usual assessment of profit potential for each segment should be completed to avoid attempting to serve unprofitable segments.

Many entrepreneurs find this approach simpler since they are required to deal with one person representing one segment at a time. Too, the segments are clearly identified with one person who allows framing marketing mixes for each segment to proceed without too much trouble.

A word of warning about picking the first segment(s) to exploit: small-business people are often enamored with big segments. Target marketing is about conserving resources and using available resources effectively and efficiently. For small businesses with limited resources, try tackling a smaller segment initially and begin generating profits and cash flow before attempting to exploit larger segments. Many small businesses lack the resources to sustain their operation until cash flow breakeven is achieved when they attempt to exploit larger segments.

A "QUICK AND DIRTY" ASSESSMENT OF BUSINESS OPPORTUNITIES

Determine early on in a venture whether additional time and money should be devoted to the project. Spending several months and several hundred dollars on a project only to discover that it is not feasible may be a waste. In assessing ventures into areas where businesses already exist, there is enough information to get a pretty good idea about whether a new business has any chance to capture an adequate market to supply the necessary revenues.

The Census of Business, including *The Census of Retail Trade, The Census of Selected Services, The Census of Wholesale Trade,* and *The Census of Manufacturing* combined with other censuses such as *The Census of Population* or other estimates of numbers of customers can be used to do a "quick and dirty" assessment of market and sales potential.

In Table 3.2 basic information about a potential flower shop in Ouachita Parish (County) was gathered. From *The Census of Retail Trade,* information on total sales and number of stores in 1997 has been gathered for the United States and Louisiana. Population data for 2000 from *The Census of the Population* has been gathered for the United States and Louisiana, and Ouachita Parish.

Data on sales and number of stores for flower shops were not available for Ouachita Parish, where the store was to be located. However, the number of people was available from the 2000 *Census of Population.* The yellow pages for the parish shows that there were twenty-one flower shops in 2004.

Using the available information, disjointed as it is in time, it is possible to calculate the average sales per store in the United States in 1997 ($250,194) and for Louisiana ($214,536). Sales per person were $23 for the United States and $20 for Louisiana.

Ouachita Parish has twenty-one stores at the present time. Using Louisiana store sales information sales can be estimated for Paul's Floral Shoppe, the proposed store. Multiplying the sales per store for

TABLE 3.2. Selected analysis of florist data.

	United States	Louisiana	Ouachita Parish
Stores[a]	26,200	407	21[b]
Total sales[a]	$6,555,088	$87,316	—
Population[c]	281,421,906	4,468,976	147,250
Average sales per store	$250,194	$214,536	—
Sales per capita	$23	$20	—
Population per store	10,741	10,980	7,012

Using Louisiana figures

	Ouachita Parish Potential	Paul's Floral Shoppe Potential
Store sales	$4,505,248	$204,784
Per capita	$2,877,008	$130,773

[a]*The Census of Business,* 1997
[b]Ouachita Parish yellow pages, 2004
[c]*The Census of Population,* 2000

Louisiana by the number of people in Ouachita Parish yields a market potential of $4,505,248 and a sales potential for Paul's Floral Shoppe of $204,784. This number was calculated by dividing the market potential by twenty-two stores. This estimate might lead one to jump right in. To verify this sales potential for Paul's, an alternate look should be made. A similar calculation using Louisiana per capita expenditures leads to an estimate of only $130,773. If that is sufficient to breakeven with debt service, the proposed venture may work.

Finally, the number of people per store in the United States was 10,741, in Louisiana was 10,980, and, in Ouachita Parish was 7,012. This latter number indicates that there are more stores in Ouachita Parish, on average based on population, than in the United States or Louisiana. This could be cause for concern.

These analyses, crude as they are, can be used without much sophistication and with available library resources to aid potential entrepreneurs in quickly eliminating clearly unfeasible projects. If this preliminary analysis shows a potentially good market, then the more detailed analysis described in the following text, which examines the market in much greater depth, should be undertaken.

MARKET FACTORS

Market factors are the realities in the market that cause the demand for the product. For example, the market factor for cribs is the number of babies born each year. Since a market is merely people with money and a motivation to buy, population figures and income figures are commonly used as market factors. However, you can be much more specific in identifying market factors for a given company or product/service. The interest in market factors is threefold: (1) to identify the factors that influence a product or service's demand, (2) determine the relationship between the factor and the product or service, and (3) forecast that market factor for future years. Since many of the same market factors are used by different forecasters, much of the forecasting work may have already been completed and simply needs to be located. Population projections, for example, are available through many sources, so there is usually no need to develop you own forecast of population. (Potential sources of data are given in Appendix A.)

Two basic techniques useful for selecting and determining the impact of market factors on a given product or service are *arbitrary judgment* and *correlation analysis.* Arbitrary judgment uses the decision maker's own experience and judgment in selection factors and weighing them. (For new products/services this is a common technique since no sales history is available unless, of course, a test market is used.) For example, a drug manufacturer might determine from historical data that $2 worth of drugs are purchased for each person residing in a given market area. The number of consumers in a market area would be used to get information on the future size of that market area.

A more complex, yet usually more reliable approach is to use correlation analysis to help identify factors and assign weights to them. Although we are not discussing the details of this technique here, another technique in correlation analysis called step-wise regression analysis not only weights the various factors but also provides a measure of what the addition of each factor adds to an explanation of changes in sales. This method requires a sales history and is limited mainly to existing products, even though it could be used on test market data for new products.

Regardless of the technique used in analyzing market factors, the basic information sought deals with understanding the factors which influence demand for a product or service and the historical and future trend of that factor. This will be more evident in the discussion of using market factors to estimate market potential in the following section.

MARKET POTENTIAL

Once a market has been divided into various segments and characteristics of consumers and market factors in each market have been analyzed, the next step is to estimate the size of the market. The term *market potential* is used to refer to the expected sales of a product or service for an entire market. More simply, "If everybody that could buy would buy, how many units or dollars worth of sales would occur?" The answer to that question is the market potential. A market segment which does not have enough consumers spending enough dollars does not justify effort in that market unless a firm is seeking to accomplish some non–revenue-related objective. You are not just seeking consumer markets, but markets that can be served profitably by the firm attempting to meet their needs. Market potential is a quantitative measure of a market's capacity to consume a product in a given time period, which is a prerequisite to assessing profitability.

ESTIMATING POTENTIAL FOR EXISTING PRODUCTS

Market potential can be measured in either absolute or relative terms. An absolute measure is one which can be expressed in units or dollars, and a relative measure relates one part of a market to another and is expressed as a percent. Techniques for estimating absolute measures of potential are discussed in the following text. These techniques are used when products and services are already on the market and the future size of the market is desired.

Sales Index Measure of Relative Potential

The sales index method provides a relative measure of potential for products that have reached the maturity stage of their product life cycle. This technique is useful in answering questions about the relative potential of various geographical market areas. Its use requires familiarity with the product in terms of stage and life cycle, penetration of distribution in various areas, and it also requires a sales history.

This technique is illustrated in the artificial product data listed in Table 3.3. Notice that the resulting figures are percentages of total industry sales by region. This, in effect, is saying that industry sales will occur next year in the same proportion as last year's in each region. The potential in the Northwest region is expected to be 23.2 percent of the total—whatever that total turns out to be next year. One region can be compared to another using this measure of potential.

Market Factor Method

Normally, relative potential is not adequate and an absolute measure of potential is needed to provide estimates of potential in units or dollars. One technique used to accomplish this is the market factor method. This involves identifying the factors which influence a good or service's sales and relating the factor to sales in some way. This was mentioned in Chapter 2. An example of this method is shown in Table 3.4, where population was used as the market factor. Population is related to sales in this example through the sales rate or dollars of sales per 1,000 people. Notice that absolute and relative potential could be calculated by region by using the projected regional population as the factor and the regional sales rate to the market factor in each region.

TABLE 3.3. Sales index method.

Region	Industry Sales	Sales Index	Potential
Northeast	$8,500,009	28.8%	28.8%
Southeast	6,753,090	22.8	22.8
Northwest	6,870,421	23.2	23.2
Southwest	7,430,218	25.2	25.2
	29,553,738	100.0%	100.0%

TABLE 3.4. The market factor method.

Region	Sales ($)	Population (000)	Sales Rate/ 1,000
Northeast	$8,500,009	68,570	$123.96
Southeast	6,753,090	38,720	174.40
Northwest	6,870,421	32,810	209.40
Southwest	7,430,218	66,730	111.34
	$29,553,738	206,830	$154.78 (avg.)

Note: Population projection (next year) = 210,847,000; Sales rate (average) = $152.78/1,000; Potential (154.78 × 210,847) = $32,634,898.

Given a market segment, the number of people in that segment, and an expenditure rate, the potential of that segment can be calculated. Using this technique produces an estimate of the absolute potential of a given market. This technique would be appropriate when an established market is being evaluated.

Regression Analysis Method

Another technique used to estimate potential involves the use of a statistical technique known as regression analysis. This technique still makes use of market factors but the market factors are related to sales in a more mathematically complex manner. Space does not permit a complete explanation of this technique. The purpose here is to show how it could be used in estimating potential. One result of regression analysis is an equation which relates the market factor to sales. If more than one market factor is used, then multiple regression is needed. Table 3.5 shows data which has been analyzed using two market factors. The resulting equation is then used to estimate potential. The approach still requires estimates of two market factors (independent variables) for the future time period for which the measure of potential is desired. In this example, Y represents total industry sales while X_1 and X_2 represent two market factors which are related to total industry sales. Estimates of the value of these factors for the next time period are substituted into the equation to calculate an estimate of industry potential. This technique also permits calculation of a confidence interval for the estimate.

TABLE 3.5. Estimating market potenial using multiple regression analysis.

Year	Industry Sales (000) Y	Factor 1 (000) X_1	Factor 2 (000) X_2
1993	6,860	1,329	40
1994	6,520	1,116	39
1995	6,345	1,041	40
1996	6,710	1,209	37
1997	7,222	1,553	44
1998	6,810	1,296	45
1999	7,005	1,365	44
2000	7,275	1,492	50
2001	7,450	1,641	53
2002	7,250	1,591	59
2003	7,105	1,510	66
2004	6,666	1,196	71
2005	6,900	1,322	72

Note: $Y = a + b_1X_1 + b_2X_2$ (general equation); $Y = 4,641 + (1.70)(1,600) + (-.46)(60)$; $Y = 7,333.4$, the estimated market potential for this product.

ESTIMATING POTENTIAL FOR NEW PRODUCTS OR SERVICES

When innovative new products or services are proposed, no industry sales are available as a point of reference for estimating potential. Under such circumstances, you should identify market factors that are likely to influence the demand for the product or service. These factors can provide an upper limit to demand.

Knowing that there were 5 million men in a certain income and age category would be a useful reference point in beginning to analyze potential for a new product for males with these two characteristics. However, you would not expect each one of them to buy the product. Three techniques commonly used to refine estimates of potential from that upper limit are: (1) judgmental estimates, (2) consumer surveys, and (3) the substitute method. A fourth technique combines several techniques and uses secondary data and consumer surveys to estimate potential.

Judgmental estimates: This involves the use of expert opinion of those knowledgeable about the market and product. This judgment can be used in a formalized approach such as the Delphi technique, which obtains a conversion over a series of tentative questions, or it could involve pooled estimates and a reconciliation of difference between estimates given by different people.

Consumer surveys: Survey of potential consumers can be used to estimate potential new products. This approach is especially useful for industrial products where the number of consumers is smaller and they can be more readily identified. For example, a part used in mud pumps for oil drilling rigs would involve only a few customers—manufacturers of mud pumps—who can be easily identified and their potential purchases of the part estimated. The more diverse consumer market makes this technique more difficult to use but it can be adapted to consumer goods.

Substitute method: Most new products are substitutes for existing products on the market. If the size of these markets can be estimated, then the sales of the new product can be estimated based on its replacement potential for existing products. An acceptance rate would have to be estimated for the proportion of existing consumers that would switch to the new product when it was introduced on the market. This acceptance rate could be estimated through consumer research.

An example of the use of combined techniques to estimate potential for a new product is shown in the following paragraphs. This example, based on actual data, shows how data from several sources can be combined to estimate market potential.

The purpose of the analysis was to evaluate the market potential for a new consumer product used in ironing. This involved evaluation of total market size and acceptance levels of this product. To accomplish these objectives, two separate phases of study were completed. Phase I was the market potential analysis based on data collected from secondary sources to estimate total market size. Phase II of the study was a consumer survey of homemakers. This survey involved collecting data from a random sample of 100 homemakers to permit more precise estimates of market potential for the product, therefore reducing the risks involved in introducing the product.

Data for the consumer study was collected by telephone interviews. The resulting data were analyzed using a computer to develop cross-tabulations of the responses. This permitted comparisons of consumers on various characteristics to assess product acceptance.

Respondents, while not representative of the total United States, were representative of consumers in the Southeast since the data were collected in that region. Market potential for the Southeastern United States was then estimated. Using information about the expected price most commonly mentioned in the consumer study produced a dollar market potential estimate of retail sales for the twelve-state region of the United States.

As this example indicates, the data collected in the consumer study were used to refine the estimates of market potential. Instead of assuming all households used ironing boards and had experienced the problems the new product would alleviate, data were collected. This permitted eliminating consumers who did not have an ironing board, did not use spray starch, did not experience specific problems, and those who said they would not be likely to buy the product if it were available. The price they would expect to pay enabled those preparing the study to estimate potential in units and dollars.

SUMMARY

The analysis of market demand discussed in this chapter lays the foundation for the analysis to be discussed in later chapters. An understanding of the market and the factors which influence the growth and size of a market are fundamental concepts for any opportunity.

This foundation is expanded in the next chapter as competitors are analyzed with respect to a product's market situation. Competitive conditions influence not only the nature of the opportunity but also provide examples of potentially successfully strategies.

Chapter 4

Competitive Analysis

After analyzing the environmental factors, market factors, potential, and the needs of consumers in specific market segments, the next step in the market opportunity analysis process is to analyze competition for each of the specific market segments. For new products that represent innovations, this analysis may be limited to potential competition rather than identifiable competitors. In most cases, however, there is an established market with clearly identified competitors who must be evaluated for their strategies, strengths, and weaknesses.

This chapter presents the concepts and tools needed to analyze competition for existing markets. Especially useful is the marketing mix audit form, which permits evaluation of a competitor in all the basic strategy elements.

PURPOSE OF COMPETITIVE ANALYSIS

One fundamental question is asked in undertaking competitive analysis: *Which competitors are going after which market segments with what marketing strategies?* The focus is again on the specific market segments that have been isolated through consumer analysis. At this point, you should already know the size (potential) and the characteristics of each segment, and now the analysis begins to deal with competition on a segment-by-segment basis. You are trying to uncover segments that are not currently being served or segments that are not being served well by competition. In markets where competitors do not have clearly identifiable strategies and each seems to be using a strategy similar to the others, there are usually several segments which can be better served through strategies aimed directly at their needs.

At one time the hair shampoo market was characterized by two broad categories of shampoo—dandruff and nondandruff. However, recognition of the different hair and scalp conditions of consumers led to the development of shampoos for dry, oily, and normal hair. This was an attempt to meet the needs of consumers more precisely than with what was previously marketed. The introduction of a shampoo especially designed for small children was an attempt to meet a need not previously met well by any competitor.

TYPES OF COMPETITION

The analysis of competition must consider *existing* and *potential* competition to be complete. Trying to anticipate the moves of the competitors can become the basis of choosing or not choosing to go after a given segment and what strategy to use if the effort is made. This chapter begins with a discussion of the nature of competition and then develops basic tools to analyze competitors.

Pure Competition

One of the earliest types of competition identified by economists is called pure competition. Although all the characteristics of this type of competition are seldom found in the marketplace, it is somewhat characteristic of some market environments and serves as a useful concept in analysis. An industry or a local market which could be described as pure competition usually has the following characteristics: (1) large number of relatively small competitors, (2) little or no differences between strategies, (3) ease of entry by new competitors. The large number of small competitors means the actions of one competitor may be unnoticed by the others. Differences among strategies may be small, and good location may be of prime importance in attracting customers. The ease of entry may mean new competitors continually coming into the market or old ones leaving. Unless a well-financed competitor enters the market and alters the competitive environment, the market tends to be unorganized, even fragmented, with the number of customers and competitors within the geographical bounds of the firm determining both sales and strategies. Similarities in prices, products or services offered, distribution, and promotion are common.

Monopolistic Competition

In the market characterized by monopolistic competition, the individual images of the various firms begin to emerge in terms of more clearly differentiated strategies. Although there may still be many competitors and relative ease of entry, each firm has attempted to differentiate itself in some way from its competitors. It may be a market with much diversity of price, distribution, products and services, and promotional activities, or it can also be characterized by similarities among two or three variables in the marketing mix and variety in the other—promotion, for example. In this competitive environment each competitor has more control over the marketing mix variables, and therefore a diversity of strategies is possible.

Oligopolistic Competition

In a competitive environment described as oligopolistic, the number of competitors and ease of entry are both decreased. A few relatively large competitors are present, and perhaps a few smaller ones too. The actions of one competitor are clearly recognized in both nature and impact by other competitors, and their retaliation to competitive moves is anticipated. Strategies in this type of environment are diverse, but it is most likely of the nonprice variety; price competition is not easily copied and must be responded to if customers readily substituted one firm's products for another. Price leadership may develop as one firm is allowed to set the price for others.

Monopoly

A monopoly is a market environment characterized by one seller. Legal restrictions are place on entry if it is considered a natural monopoly (telephone company, electric utility company, etc.). Natural monopolies are regulated by government in terms of prices and distribution, and nonnatural monopolies, if successful, usually attract other competitors who are willing to overcome barriers to entry because of a potentially large return. Therefore, nonnatural monopolies are usually short-lived.

LEVEL OF COMPETITION

One important aspect of competition that must be understood is the level at which it is analyzed. At the manufacturing level, there may be only a few large producers (oligopoly) but many retailers reselling the products in highly competitive markets (monopolistic or purely competitive). Therefore, the planner must analyze the market in terms of where his or her own firm faces competition. If the marketing plan is being developed for a retail firm, the retail market is of prime consideration, whereas a manufacturer may be more concerned about competition at the manufacturing level.

In some instances it may be appropriate to look at competition vertically, with one channel system competing with another channel system, rather than only horizontally. This would be especially true where vertical integration is involved.

DECIDING ON THE NATURE
OF THE COMPETITION

Table 4.1 provides a summary of the variation of several factors depending on the type of competitive environment that is appropriate. This table is useful in understanding the nature of the competitive environment. Instead of trying to define what is meant by "many" in the case of number of firms, and "ease of entry" in the case of how easy it is to enter a market, attention should be focused on the overall nature of the market as described by the factors *collectively*. Since most of economic reality lies somewhere between pure competition and monopoly, attention should be focused on the analysis. Identifying the nature of competition helps in understanding not only how firms compete in a market but also whether or not retaliatory actions can be expected.

COMPETITIVE ADVANTAGES

Effective competitive analysis will take into consideration the search for, and need for, differential advantages. Differential advantages are those factors in which a particular organization excels over competitive organizations or has the potential to excel over them.

TABLE 4.1. Effects of the competitive environment.

Factor	Pure Competition	Monopolistic Competition	Oligopolistic Competition	Monopoly
Number of firms	Many	Many	Few	One
Entry and exit	Easy	Easy	Difficult	May be banned
Product	Undifferentiated	Differentiated	Differentiated	NA
Price	Undifferentiated	Undifferentiated if non-price competition is emphasized. Differentiated if price competition is used by some competitors.	Differentiated if nonprice competition is emphasized. Differentiated if price competition is used by some competitors.	NA
Place	Undifferentiated	Differentiated if non-price competition is used by some competitors. Undifferentiated if price competition is emphasized.	Differentiated if nonprice competition is used by some competitors. Undifferentiated if price competition is emphasized.	NA
Promotion	Undifferentiated	Differentiated if non-price competition is used by some competitors. Undifferentiated if price competition is emphasized.	Differentiated if nonprice competition is used by some competitors. Undifferentiated if price competition is emphasized.	NA
Competitive reactions	Little	Some, depending on type of action.	A lot, especially price action.	NA

Some strategic planners actually insist that a result of the strategic planning process must be some differential advantage for the organization. Differential advantages may be found in the areas of production, technology, natural resources, marketing, and management.

1. *Production:* A superior ability to turn out a product is a critical differential advantage that many companies have capitalized upon. The advantage may also be in a firm's ability to maintain superior production quality over competitors.
2. *Technology:* Initial innovative research and development, as well as properly managed scientific application, can establish and preserve strong differential advantages over competitors.
3. *Natural resources:* Quite often valuable or scarce resources are appropriate assets on which to base a strategy. Tremendous advantage can be given to organizations, cartels, and nations that control natural resources or who are located in favorable proximity to them.
4. *Marketing:* Market advantage usually refers to the advantage one firm has over another because it is more positively positioned in the minds of customers. Those having greater awareness, higher preference, or stronger loyalty have distinct marketing differential advantage over their competitors.
5. *Management:* Management advantage comes in the form of positive personnel relations, effective planning and information systems, and overall managerial competence.

INDUSTRY ANALYSIS

Part of the competitive analysis process is to discover differential advantages that will enhance the strategy of the firm. To discover these differences one must understand how the industry functions. The following four key questions are helpful in conducting an industry analysis.

1. How is the industry structured?
2. What is the industry's direction?
3. What are the industry economics?
4. What are the strategic issues within the industry?[1]

The analysis of the *industry structure* involves determining the number of competitors, establishing their size relative to the total market, profiling the market leaders, analyzing distribution channels, developing consumer profiles, and evaluating ease of entry and exit as well as other characteristics.

Once the industry framework is understood the analysis turns toward determining the *industry's direction*. Most industries go through an industry life cycle consisting of the development stage, the growth stage, the maturity stage, and the decline stage. However, this model of understanding and predicting industry direction is not always accurate. Some industries go through several cycles. The checklist in Exhibit 4.1 includes many of the considerations required to answer the question of where the industry is going and what is driving it that way.

Many other driving forces are present. Various industries will have different forces that help determine the direction of the industry and the forces will have different magnitudes of importance from one industry to another.

The forces of competition greatly influence the strategy formation and market opportunity decisions of an organization. Although each industry has its own unique characteristics, five main forces are representative of the actual driving mechanisms of any given industry. These forces, shown in Figure 4.1, are:

1. The industry itself and the competitive decisions and activities engaged in by each company
2. Consumer/buyer composition
3. Supplier composition
4. The possibility of new entrants
5. Availability of good product substitutes[2]

The *industry* and the individual companies within the industry are constantly involved in dynamic interplay in an attempt to build a successful competitive edge over one another. The success of one organization's strategy in accomplishing this is based in large measure on the strategies of the other members. Constant monitoring of these interdependent strategic maneuvers is required to make the adjustments necessary to improve competitive position and achieve market success.

EXHIBIT 4.1. Industry direction checklist.

	Slow	Medium	Fast
1. Growth	____	____	____
	Growing	Declining	No change
2. Customers	____	____	____
	Low	Medium	High
3. Technology	____	____	____
	Slow	Medium	Fast
4. Product change	____	____	____
	Low	Medium	High
5. Danger of obsolescence	____	____	____
	Low	Medium	High
6. Ease of entry	____	____	____
	Low	Medium	High
7. Quality of suppliers	____	____	____
	Low	Medium	High
8. Possibility of regulatory changes	____	____	____
	Low	Medium	High
9. Availability of rawmaterials/ resources	____	____	____
	Low	Medium	High
10. Amount of capital required	____	____	____

Consumer/buyer composition can range from a few, high-volume purchasers to a large number of low-volume purchasers. In one instance losing a few customers can be the difference between success and failure, and at the other extreme losing the same number of customers has essentially no impact. Most firms try to minimize the number of customers that can exert an adverse effect on their business.

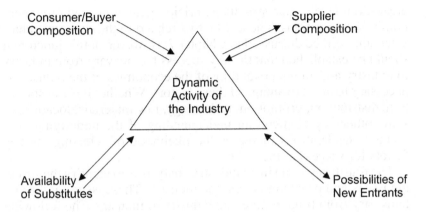

FIGURE 4.1. Competitive forces model. *Source:* Adapted from Michael E. Porter, "How Competitive Forces Shape Strategy," *Harvard Business Review,* 57, No. 2 (March-April 1979), p. 141.

Supplier composition also has an important influence on the competing position of individual organizations. The relative importance of the goods or services they supply will determine the strength of their competitive influence over firms in the industry. They can have a positive or negative impact on profit margins, inventory levels, product quality, and prices.

The *possibility of new entrants* into the market is a constant threat to altering market share, production capacity, and supply distribution within the industry. This threat can be minimal when there are strong barriers to entry such as strong customer loyalty, large capital requirements, difficulty in establishing distribution channels, and strong response of current market participants. When entry barriers are weak or expected response of existing firms is weak then the possibility of entry is stronger.

The fifth force in the model is the *availability of good product substitutes*. This is a major threat to existing firms when high-quality substitutes exist in ample quantity at competitive or comparable prices. Aspartame and sugar are examples of substitutable products.

The third key question in accomplishing a competitive analysis is "What are the underlying economics of the industry?" The elements required to answer this question are capital investment requirements, break-even levels, cost structures, pricing structures, and other economic considerations. The key factors related to the economic characteristics will be discussed in Chapter 7. However, at this juncture it should be established that the key success factors vary from industry to industry and an understanding of the economics of the industry is necessary to take advantage of these factors. Whether it is transportation, distribution, promotion, technology, raw materials, location, or some other key element, an understanding of the underlying economic considerations increases the likelihood of selecting the key factors for success in the industry.

The fourth key issue in an industry analysis is to identify the strategic issues and problems facing the industry. These issues and problems vary from time to time and industry to industry. The following are the most common issues and problems within an industry.

1. Capability of meeting future needs.
2. Ability to estimate changes of the demographic characteristics of consumers.
3. Capacity to deal with emerging opportunities and threats.
4. Ability to trace the overall economy and estimate its impact on the industry.
5. Ability to anticipate changes in government policies and regulatory controls.
6. Capability to predict and respond to changes in supply, cost, competition, technology, and growth.

COMPETITOR ANALYSIS

Once a good understanding is established of how the industry functions, a specific competitor analysis is called for. Most firms in a given industry do not follow the same strategic approach regardless of the similarity of their understanding of the dynamics of the industry. Evaluating the competitors' strategy in the market allows a business entity to increase or reinforce its understanding of buyer behavior and identify the type of customer being appealed to. It also helps identify strengths and weaknesses and consequently potential market opportunity. The analysis may assist the firm in evaluating whether to position itself as a *leader* competing head-on with other competitors, as a *follower* with a "me-too" strategy, or as a *niche* performer with a unique strategy tailored for specific strengths and weaknesses and specific market segments.

In evaluating different competitive approaches, the following considerations need to be made:

- Review current strategy.
- Review current performance.
- Determine strengths and weakness.
- Forecast future strategic possibilities.

Each major competitor should be studied separately. If this is not possible then the strategy of the closest competitors should be evaluated.

Analyzing current competitor strategy involves determining how the competitor defines the industry in terms of market segments, product features, marketing mix, manufacturing policy, research and development commitment, growth policy, distribution, and promotion. This analysis can take several forms, but perhaps the most useful is the competitive market-mix audit.

THE COMPETITIVE MARKET-MIX AUDIT

The competitive market-mix audit is one of the best ways of evaluating the marketing performance of a company and its competitors.[3] An audit of this nature should be comprehensive, independent, and periodic. The audit should be based on specific objectives. Once the objectives and scope of the audit are established, a data-gathering effort should be initiated. This data-collection effort can be accomplished by an objective outside consultant or by an in-house staff or task force. The results of the audit should be a clear comparison of the company and its competitors, which shows relative strengths and weaknesses as well as opportunities and threats. Other possible outcomes include the detection of inappropriate objectives, obsolete strategy, ill-advised use of resources, and other needs for revising the direction of the company relative to competition.

The word *audit*, regardless of the business context it is used in, refers to an unbiased appraisal of what is being done and how it is being done. Thus an accounting audit refers to an analysis of everything that is being done in the accounting area of a firm. In the same manner, a competitive market-mix audit is an analysis of competitors' activities by market segment. The form shown in Table 4.2 is one of the most useful tools available for performing such an audit for a retail company. Other audit forms with different comparison characteristics should be used for other industry categories. The audit involves the planner in an appraisal of every aspect of a firm's marketing mix compared to that of its major competitors. Several steps are involved in using this form to complete the audit.

First, the form should reflect the nature of the market-mix activities for the type of firms being analyzed. For example, if retail firms are being analyzed, the form must reflect the components important in retailing. Specifically, place would be analyzed in terms of appearance, layout, and traffic flows throughout the stores. This analysis would not be appropriate for a manufacturer since customers do not usually see the physical facility or move through it.

Second, the major competitors must be identified by name so that a realistic comparison can be made. This requirement forces the planner to identify the specific competitors going after a market segment and permits the collection of data on those specific firms.

Third, sources of data must be identified to complete the audit. Some of the data may already be available from previous analysis or research and merely need updating. Or data may have to be collected to complete the audit. For some types of comparisons, judgment must be used if research or other objective data are not available. The danger is for a "halo effect" on what you are doing compared to competitors. One way to avoid bias is to use the judgment of several people rather than relying on that of one person.

The first, a minus sign, indicates that the business being evaluated ranks below the competitor on the specific factor; the second, a question mark, indicates that the relative standing is unknown; the third, a zero, indicates equal competitive standing; and the fourth, a plus sign, indicates that the business being evaluated ranks above the competition on the specific factor.

Finally, develop a system to "grade" your own company's effort and competitors on each aspect of the audit. For new firms anticipating entry into a market, competitors are compared with each other. The ranking system previously described is one possibility. In this system, each competitor is ranked as to whether it is perceived

TABLE 4.2. Competitive market-mix audit form.

	Comp. A – ? 0 +	Comp. B – ? 0 +	Comp. C. – ? 0 +
Product or Service			
1. Customer acceptance			
2. Customer satisfaction in use			
3. Product quality level(s)/innovations			
4. Adequacy of assortments			
5. Services provided			
Place			
1. Customer accessibility			
2. Suitability of site for			
3. Customer traffic potential			
4. Appearance of facility			
5. Selling areas			
6. Parking facilities			
7. Drawing power of neighboring firms			
8. Customer image of facilities			
Price			
1. Comparative price level(s)			
2. Consumers' images of store's prices			
3. Number of price lines			
4. Consistency of price policies			
5. Credit policies and practices			
Promotion			
1. Promotional ability			
2. Amount and quality of promotional efforts in			
3. Ethical standards			
4. Consistency of efforts			

Source: Adapted from C. H. McGregor and Paul C. Chakmas, *Retail Management Problems,* Fourth Edition, Homewood, IL: Richard D. Irwin, Inc., 1970, pp. 255-256.

"higher," "lower," "equal to," or "don't know" on each part of the audit. Or one could rank competitors in order using 1 to indicate the best, 2 the second best, and so on.

Rather than a more general analysis of price levels, this audit would need to be completed for *each segment* analyzed. The planner is not particularly interested in the generalities here but rather the details about specific groups or segments in the market. Be thorough in this type of analysis. Lack of digging into the details may even be misleading.

In a consumer study done for a restaurant, respondents were asked whether they thought their friends would eat at that particular restaurant. If the answer was no, they were asked why. The most common response was that prices were "too high." Yet the competitive analysis of fictitious restaurants listed in Table 4.3 tells a completely different story. The prices charged by the Holliday Restaurant were about the same as the other competitors for comparable menu items, which means respondents *thought* the prices were too high. This problem leads to a completely different type of strategy or tactics than if prices were in fact higher than those of competitors.

TABLE 4.3. Competitive pricing in restaurants.

	8-oz. Rib Eye	Hamburger w/Fries	Breakfast	Buffet	Banquet
Southern Inn	$7.26	$3.50	$1.95	$3.95	$6.50
King's Inn	3.70	2.05	—	—	—
Charlie's Place	7.68	—	—	—	—
Tony's	6.84	3.25	1.75	—	5.25
Sandpiper	6.49	3.00	1.75	—	6.00
The Castle	7.96	3.60	1.85	—	On request
Ramble Inn	6.20	3.05	1.80	—	7.95
The Rib Joint	6.88	2.55	1.75	—	6.50-7.50
The Ice Box	7.16	3.40	—	—	6.50
Uncle Joe's	7.87	2.25	—	—	6.50
Captain Bill's	7.95	2.95	—	—	—
John's Diner	7.50	2.85	—	4.95	6.35
Holliday Restaurant	7.25	2.75	1.95	4.95	6.50

COMPETITIVE STRATEGIES AND RESOURCES

Several other factors should be analyzed for a more complete evaluation of competitors in a market. They include competitors' strategic tendencies and resources—marketing, financial, and production. These relate to long-run actions as opposed to short run.

The first factor is concerned with competitors' willingness to change or react to competitive moves; the second deals with their ability to make strategic moves.

Assessing strategic tendencies involves deciding whether competitors' actions tend to be reactive or proactive. Reactive strategies are those which follow the lead of other firms in the market or simply settle into a niche. Proactive strategies involve market leadership or challenge to the market leaders. If market leaders and challengers can be identified, they are the competitors whose actions must be anticipated. The market-mix audit of these firms helps identify the exact nature of their strategies in a short approach.

A strategy used by many firms in recent years is called product positioning—the placement of a product in terms of consumers' perceptions of it relative to other products. It answers the question, "How do we want consumers to perceive our product relative to other products on the market?" The market mix is altered in an attempt to put that product in that position in the minds of consumers.

If the market for a product could be viewed as a multidimensional plane, all attributes of a product together make up its position. For simplicity, however, one or two key dimensions are usually chosen for analysis. For example, the "product space" for brands of bar soap could represent two dimensions: the extent to which consumers perceive the soaps to moisturize and deodorize their skin. Zest and Safeguard have long-occupied the quadrant of high moisturizing/deodorant. When Lever introduced its new brand, Lever 2000, it was positioned in between these older brands and carved out a very healthy segment of the market because it more closely met the needs of a large cluster of customers.

Assessing competitors' resources involves determining whether specific competitors have the marketing expertise to respond successfully to events in the marketplace, the productive capacity to respond in terms of both levels of demand and technology, and finally, the financial resources to respond to problems and opportunities that occur. Moreover, since most firms attempt to build on their strengths and nullify their weaknesses, analysis can help them forecast the type of response they are most likely to make. A firm that is strong financially with unused productive capacity but weaker marketing skills is most likely to meet a challenge with lower prices or an increase in promotional expenditures than would a firm with an opposite set of strengths and weaknesses.

As the market moves toward oligopolistic competition, the necessity of this type of analysis becomes more significant. Failure to expect and anticipate competitive reactions is to ignore the realities of market dynamics.

After completing the competitive analysis by market segment, develop summary statements about each segment with respect to competition.

SEARCH FOR A DIFFERENTIAL ADVANTAGE

As each competitive firm's strategy, strengths, and weaknesses are analyzed for each market segment, the market analyst is looking for those segments not being served or not being served well by existing competition. Successful entry and exploitation of a marketing opportunity is much easier if a firm finds some differential advantage in the market. *A differential advantage gives one firm an edge over competitors and becomes a basis of differentiating one firm from another in the market.* The basis of the advantage could be price, product improvement, promotional appeals, product innovation, etc.[4]

When this approach is used, the analyst begins to interpret "holes in the market" in terms of his or her own firm's ability to fill that niche. Thus opportunities and abilities are matched. (This matching process is examined in more detail in Chapter 7.)

POSITIONING THE COMPANY/PRODUCT

One you have adequately analyzed and assessed the competition, it is time to formulate the strategy to position your product, company, or SBU based on the competitive analysis. Most companies will be either a market leader, a market challenger, a market follower, or a market nicher.[5]

Market leaders occupy first place by way of market share for a particular product or product line. They establish strategy to maintain their number one position. Their objectives usually are to expand total market usage of the product, to protect their current market share.

Market challengers occupy the second, third, or fourth place in market share (depending on the size of the market and the number of competitors). Although not as large as market leaders, these firms are usually quite large in their own right. Market challengers also seek to gain market share. They attempt to accomplish this by frontal assaults or flanking movements specifically against the market leaders. The flanking strategies are generally preferred because they represent a concentration of effort against an identified area of weakness in the leader. Market challengers can also meet their objectives by attacking smaller competitors rather than the market leader. This is sometimes referred to as a "guppy strategy."

Market followers seldom choose to make frontal or head-on attacks on market leaders. Because of their smaller size and their less aggressive philosophy, market followers usually employ flanking or guppy strategies in the competitive arena.

Market nichers are smaller companies which appeal to a particular segment of the market based on their unique strengths. Their strategies usually do not include head-on clashes with market leaders or market challengers for that matter. The market nichers usually capitalize on an area of specialization or specific market segment which large companies tend to overlook or ignore.

Successful positioning of the company/product, therefore, begins with an understanding of a company's market position in the competitive market as well as a broad-based knowledge of the company's strengths, weaknesses, and capabilities. This allows the company to stake out a position that will lead to long-term growth. Often this will require making product innovations, creating positive relationships with key suppliers and customers, establishing consumer awareness, and developing internal efficiencies and competence.

SUMMARY

At this point in the analysis, the analyst should begin to see several clear-cut problems and opportunities in the market. Not only have general and specific characteristics of the market been analyzed but also the responses of competitive firms that are pursuing these markets.

For new firms in a market, the competitive analysis has another advantage. Because the other firms have already adjusted to market conditions with their own strategies, their own approaches to the market are suggestive of successful and unsuccessful ways to enter and compete in it. Their trials and errors should become a guide to avoiding mistakes already made and activities already proven unsuccessful either by their nature or by the way they were carried out by existing firms.

PART III:
FINANCIAL ANALYSIS

Chapter 5

Revenue and Cost Analysis

After the external analysis has been completed, the next step in business assessment is the financial analysis of the specific opportunity. Regardless of the decision-making situation involved, the financial analysis should contain at least three types of analysis: (1) revenue analysis, (2) cost analysis, and (3) analysis of return on investment (ROI).

One of the most beneficial ways to combine these three types of analyses is to utilize the concept of a pro forma income statement as the basic document to be generated by the financial analysis. A pro forma income statement is a projected income statement for a specific future time period using estimates of the revenues and costs associated with that time period. It provides an estimate of future cash flows to be produced by a given market or business opportunity which can be discounted to determine the present value of these cash flows. This, in turn, is used in calculating the rate of return anticipated as achievable from a given opportunity.

A pro forma income statement for a proposed business opportunity is shown in Table 5.1. The approach used for this venture was to develop three alternate statements, each based on a different assumption about revenues generated by the new venture. This approach permits identifying the "most optimistic," "most pessimistic," and the "most likely" outcome of a given situation. This is also a more realistic approach to demand forecasting, which produces a range of sales volume for a new product. When products or services have already been on the market for several years, industry sales history is available to use in projecting sales.

Revenue and costs can change radically over the course of a product's life cycle. For example, high investments in promotion and building distribution produce losses in early years; while, on the other hand, reduced variable costs achieved by increasing production effi-

TABLE 5.1. Pro forma income statement.

	Low (Pessimistic)	Medium (Most Likely)	High (Optimistic)
Sales	$3,500,000	$4,500,000	$5,500,000
Cost of sales	2,500,000	3,400,000	4,300,000
Gross margin	$1,000,000	$1,100,000	$1,200,000
Expenses			
Direct selling	457,000	480,000	512,000
Advertising	157,000	168,000	180,000
Transportation and storage	28,000	38,000	48,000
Depreciation	15,000	15,000	15,000
Credit and collections	12,000	14,000	16,000
Financial and clerical	29,000	38,000	47,000
Administrative	55,000	55,000	55,000
Total expenses	$753,000	$808,000	$873,000
Profit before taxes	$247,000	$292,000	$327,000
Net profit after taxes	$128,440	$151,840	$170,040
Cash flow (NPAT + Depr.)	$143,440	$166,840	$185,040

ciency and technological improvement may produce high profit levels in later years. Consequently, any realistic financial analysis must take into consideration an adequate time frame and associated changes in cost structures.

Since the financial analysis of a business assessment is usually long run in nature, either the pro forma must be estimated for each year for some assumed length of time or an "average" year can be used which represents three to five years into the future. Then the discounted cash flow from this year is used as an average for the venture's anticipated life to calculate the ROI or break-even point of the project.

If subjective probabilities are assigned to each alternative, then decision tree analysis can be used to calculate an expected value for the cash flow from the project. Otherwise, the ROI can be calculated for each alternative and then compared with a predetermined rate to evaluate the financial impact of each alternative.

Developing a pro form income statement requires a forecast of both expected revenues and operating expenses. The procedures for developing each of these estimates are discussed later in this chapter.

Thus, the revenue analysis produces an estimate of revenues, the costs analysis produces an estimate of the costs associated with those revenues, and the analysis of ROI or break-even point relates those returns to the investment to be made in the venture. This, in turn, provides the answer to the basic question posed in financial analysis: "What is the projected financial impact of pursuing this particular business or market opportunity?"

NONPROFIT FINANCIAL ANALYSIS

Many nonprofit organizations fail to apply this basic approach of opportunity assessment to their decision making. A large hospital, for example, decided to build a new wing for geriatric outpatients to provide rehabilitation services for patients suffering from major traumas such as strokes or heart attacks. The facility was built and opened to accommodate 100 patients. However, when it opened, only two patients showed up to take advantage of the new facility. An analysis of demand for such services prior to their provision would have avoided such a costly mistake.

Although the analysis of returns from a decision made by a nonprofit organization uses different criteria, such an evaluation should be made nonetheless. This type of analysis is simply an application of a basic management concept—evaluate the impact of a decision *before* you make it. This principle applies to nonprofit as well as profit-oriented organizations.

FORECASTING MARKET SHARE

Once the size of the total market has been estimated and the competition analyzed, the next step in the new product/opportunity assessment process is to estimate the sales revenue the opportunity can be expected to generate on an annual basis. The point is not trying to determine how many consumers will buy a product or service, but how many will buy *your* offering of that product or service.

For established markets, this involves estimating market share. The question is: "What share of total sales can we reasonably expect to attain?" The percent is then converted to a dollar amount—the sales revenue expected in a given time period. The key element in the estimate at this point is judgment. (If a test market is used later in the development process, this estimate can be reevaluated for soundness.)

This judgment is based on an analysis of your offering versus competitive offerings. If four competitors are in the market and your product is expected to compete on an equal footing with other offerings, then a 20 percent market share should be used as an initial estimate of market share. This basic estimate would then be raised or lowered to reflect competitive strengths and weaknesses in the market.

For new products and services not currently on the market, an acceptance rate must be estimated. The acceptance rate is the proportion of the segment that will buy your product or use your service. Two approaches can be used to estimate the acceptance rate: judgment estimates and consumer surveys.

Judgment estimates. One way to estimate the acceptance rate is to use judgment. After careful analysis of the market, the person preparing the feasibility study sets the rate, in conjunction with other people who are knowledgeable about the market. Such an "educated guess" can be effective if people who are knowledgeable about a market— retailers, wholesalers, industrial users—are consulted. This estimate also reflects what the company can bring to the market in terms of marketing skills and innovation, brand equity, and the like.

Consumer surveys. Another approach to estimating the proportion of consumers who would buy a new offering is a survey of potential consumers. Data obtained in this way have been referred to as "iffy" data—"I would buy your product *if* it were offered on the market and *if* I were in THE market at that time, and *if.* . . ." Although purchase intent statements in survey research cannot be taken completely at face value, various methods of discounting stated purchase intent are available to reflect realistic estimates of actual purchase behavior which can be expected in the marketplace. For industrial users, however, surveys with purchase decision makers can be highly effective since they are in a position to more judiciously evaluate the use of a product than many individual consumers.

These two approaches are often combined to provide a sales forecast. A set of assumptions—about market acceptance, competitive reactions, economic conditions, degree of distribution, and promotion—must also be developed as a basis for the forecast. These assumptions must precede the actual dollar forecast used in the pro forma income statement.

An example of how these approaches can be combined to estimate sales revenue is shown in Table 5.2. This table shows the estimates of attendance at a proposed miniature golf facility. Assumptions were made about the penetration or acceptance rates by the market segment and the number of repeat visitors that could be expected.

The admissions charge was anticipated to be $5 per person, giving the following alternative sales forecasts:

Low forecast	$944,000	(188,800 × $5)
Most likely	$1,077,500	(215,500 × $5)
High forecast	$1,336,000	(267,200 × $5)

A sales range of about $950,000 to $1,340,000 was estimated. To derive a figure for the pro forma income statement, the following probabilities were assigned to each forecast:

Low Forecast	.25
Most Likely	.50
High Forecast	.25

The expected value of sales revenue was then computed as follows:

$$EVSR = (\$944,000)\,(.25) + (\$1,077,500)\,(.50)$$
$$+ (\$1,336,000)\,(.25)$$
$$EVSR = \$1,108,750$$

This final value ($1,108,750) was used as the estimated sales revenue to be generated from attendance sales in the pro forma income statement.

TABLE 5.2. Attendance projections.

Facts/Assumptions	Attendance Alternate Forecasts		
	Low	Most Likely	High
Attendance/penetration			
(a) Local market population	520,000	520,000	520,000
Target market (Ages 10-25)	120,000	120,000	120,000
Penetration	.65	.70	.85
Attendance	78,000	84,000	102,000
(b) Local market			
General population	110,000	110,000	110,000
Penetration	.03	.05	.07
Attendance	3,300	5,500	7,700
(c) Regional market			
Population	100,000	100,000	100,000
Penetration	.10	.15	.20
Attendance	10,000	15,000	20,000
(d) Tourist market			
Population	250,000	250,000	250,000
Penetration	.03	.05	.07
Attendance	7,500	12,500	17,500
(e) Group sales market			
Attendance	18,000	20,500	25,000
(f) Repeat business			
Attendance	72,000	78,000	95,000
Total Attendance (Sum of a-f)	188,800	215,500	267,200

COST ANALYSIS

The bottom line of any operation or project is significantly affected by the underlying cost structure. Consequently, cost analysis is closely allied with revenue analysis. Once revenue estimates have been made, cost analysis must be carefully considered. The rest of this chapter will discuss various cost concepts, types of costs, cost information sources, cost sensitivity analysis, cost forecasting, and technical analysis.

COST CONCEPTS

Accounting for the costs of conducting business operations is complex. This is also true of analyzing costs for market opportunity assessment. As a business functions, assets lose their original identity. The business operation converts the assets into some other form. For example, raw materials of many kinds may go into a final manufactured product and many of these raw materials may be unrecognizable in the end product. Costs, however, are traced through the business operations as the assets and resources are converted into goods and services. Since the profits and losses of a business are measured as the difference between the *revenue* received from customers and the *costs* associated with the delivery of the products or services, a project cannot be judged as feasible or profitable without dependable cost estimates.

TYPES OF COSTS

Costs must be selectively chosen to match the purpose for which they are used. Care must be taken to understand the specific application of a cost under consideration.

Costs can be divided into several major categories, some of which will be very instrumental in developing the project cost summary discussed later in the chapter.

1. *Period costs:* Period costs are associated with and measured according to time intervals rather than goods or services. For example, equipment rental may be at the rate of $1,200 a month. Regardless of the amount of business or product supported by the equipment, the rental cost of the equipment remains $1,200 each month. This expense amount is allocated against revenue according to the time interval without regard to the amount of business transacted. Equipment expense for the year will show

$14,400 on the income statement. Generally speaking, selling and administrative costs are designated as period costs.

2. *Product costs:* In some cases it is inappropriate to classify costs as period costs. Some situations in the income determination process call for costs to be offset as expenses against the activity, good, or service that produced the revenue. Under this concept of income determination, the period in which the benefit is received is the period in which the costs should be expressed and deducted as expenses. Following our equipment rental example, the equipment rental for a certain period should not be charged off as rent expense for that period if the goods produced by the equipment are not sold until a later period. If costs of this type are handled as product costs, they are matched against the revenue generated from their sale in the period of that sale. In most cases, manufacturing costs are treated as product costs rather than period costs and are included in the cost of goods sold.

3. *Fixed costs:* Expenses that are expected to remain constant over a period of time regardless of activity level are called fixed costs. Examples of this type of cost are executive salaries, interest charges, rent, insurance, equipment leases, depreciation, engineering and technical support, and product development expense. Obviously, a fixed cost, as with any other cost, can be increased or decreased, particularly in an inflationary period. These variations, however, are caused by other external factors and not caused by the firm's output or activity.

Fixed costs can be broken down further as committed fixed costs and discretionary fixed costs. Various management decisions may commit the company to a course of action that will require the company to conform to a certain payment schedule for a number of years in the future. Costs incurred in this way are committed fixed costs. The costs related to acquiring a new building are examples of committed costs. On the other hand, discretionary fixed costs are established as a part of a budget that can be altered by management action on a monthly, quarterly, or yearly basis. These costs are easier to alter, and have a high degree of flexibility. Examples of discretionary fixed costs are the research and development budget or supervisory salaries that are set by management action.

4. *Variable and semivariable costs:* Costs that vary closely with production are considered variable costs. In the strictest sense of the term, variable costs should vary in direct proportion to changes in production levels. Direct material cost and direct labor costs are good examples of variable costs. Most costs, however, are semivariable. Semivariable costs may fluctuate with volume, but not in a direct relationship to production. Market research expense, advanced research expense, advertising and sales promotion expense, supplies expense, and maintenance expenses are all examples of semivariable expenses. In some cases, semivariable costs can be broken down into fixed and variable components to make application for decision making possible.

5. *Direct and indirect costs:* Direct costs are those identifiable with a particular product, activity, or department. Indirect costs are not directly identifiable with any particular product, activity, or department. Often, the distinction between direct and indirect costs depends upon the unit under consideration. A cost of specific supplies used may be identified directly as a cost of a particular department but may not be a direct cost of the product manufactured. When a cost can be directly identified to the unit under consideration, it is considered a direct cost relative to that unit. When a cost is associated with a unit only through allocation, it is an indirect cost.

6. *Controllable and noncontrollable costs:* As with direct and indirect costs, a reference point is required to classify costs as controllable or noncontrollable. Obviously, at some point in the organizational structure, all costs are controllable. Top management can dispose of property, eliminate personnel, terminate research projects, or whatever is necessary to control costs. For middle- and lower-level management, however, costs can be termed uncontrollable. If a specific level of management has the authority to authorize certain costs, then these costs are considered controllable at that level. A plant manager, for example, may have control over the supplies used by his or her plant, but he or she may have no control of promotional costs established by central headquarters.

7. *Sunk costs:* A sunk cost is usually a cost that was spent in the past and is irrelevant to a decision under consideration. This

concept will be discussed further in Chapter 6 in regard to the capital budgeting decision. Sunk costs may be variable or fixed.

8. *Differential costs:* The purpose of cost analysis is to provide management with the data necessary to compare alternatives and make a choice. In order to simplify the comparison of alternatives, any costs that remain the same regardless of the alternative will be disregarded in the analysis. A difference in cost between one course of action and another is referred to as a differential cost. In most cases the decision will result in an increased cost. This increased differential cost is often specifically referred to as an incremental cost. Differential costs are often referred to as marginal costs when the deferential cost is the additional cost required to produce one more units of a product.

9. *Opportunity costs:* Ordinarily, costs are viewed as outlays or expenditures that must be made to obtain goods and services. The concept of opportunity costs extends this to include sacrifices that are made by foregoing benefits or returns. An opportunity cost takes into consideration the fact that choosing one of several alternatives precludes receiving the benefits of the rejected alternatives. The sacrifice of a return from a rejected alternative is referred to as the opportunity cost of the chosen alternative.

Many of the costs discussed here above are overlapping in nature. Thus fixed cost may also be a sunk cost, an uncontrollable cost, or a period cost. Judgment must be used in identifying specific costs in the development of cost estimates for a specific opportunity or business venture.

DATA SOURCES

Many sources of data are found in a company's historical records. These records can provide cost information to establish reasonable cost estimates. Many other sources of data can provide information to form the basis of a reliable cost forecast. Examples include:

- *Trade publications:* These provide comparative financial ratios, cost of goods sold information, gross margin data, and other information.
- *Time studies:* These establish standards for estimating labor cost.

- *Experiments:* These test processes in terms of time, material, labor, and other resources necessary to complete production processes.
- *Pilot plant or process activities:* These involve the intermittent or continuous operation of a new plant activity or process to perfect engineering specifications and to establish cost standards.
- *Historical cost data:* This can include past material cost, labor cost, overhead expense, administrative costs, utility expense, and many other categories of expense.
- *Interviews:* These include personal interviews, telephone interviews, and mail interviews designed to gather data that provide primary cost information unavailable from other sources.

Other Sources

- *Agricultural statistics* (www.usda.gov). U.S. Department of Agriculture, Washington, DC: U.S. Government Printing Office. This resource includes statistical data concerning prices and supply of agriculturally related items.
- *Business Periodical Index.* New York: H. W. Wilson, Co. Most major libraries will have available this resource index to periodicals with an author-subject approach to areas of business interest.
- *Department of Commerce* (www.doc.gov). The regional offices of the Department of Commerce have resource libraries and extensive stores that provide a large amount of resource information for forecasting purposes.
- *Standard & Poor's* (www.standardandpoors.com). S & P also provides special in-depth coverage in reports of specific areas such as the recreation industry, entertainment industry, and so forth.
- *Standard & Poor's Industry Surveys* (www.netadvantage. standardandpoors.com). New York: McGraw-Hill, Inc. These surveys provide overall statistical data and outlook for various industries.
- *Survey of Buying Power.* New York: Sales Management. Data such as population figures, income figures, and retail sales figures are provided for specific areas of the country.

- *Thomas Register* (www.thomasnet.com). New York: Thomas Publishing Co. This series includes products and services, company addresses, and company personnel.
- *Various Census Reports:* (www.census.gov). Available for various types of activities such as construction, wholesale trade, housing, manufacturing, and transportation.
- *Wholesale prices and price indexes* (http://www.bls.gov). Washington, DC: U.S. Bureau of Labor Statistics. This report periodically provides statistical representation of various prices.

See Appendix A for further sources of information. Although Internet addresses are provided for many of the sources cited, the reader should be aware that the Web is ever-changing. Thus, some sites listed may no longer be accurate.

COST BEHAVIOR, SENSITIVITY ANALYSIS, AND RISK ANALYSIS

Before moving on to the actual development of detailed cost forecasts, a discussion of sensitivity analysis is in order. Sensitivity analysis is a technique that illustrates how the costs of an operation or activity will be affected by changes in variables or by errors in the input data. Sensitivity analysis is sometimes called "what if" analysis, because it asks and answers questions such as, "What if labor cost increases an average of $1.75/hour?" or "What if sales fall to 350,000 units?"

Other questions that can be answered include, "What happens to profits if you change selling price?" or "What happens to profits if you buy more efficient equipment, change your formulation and accompanying cost structure, or increase or decrease personnel?" The starting point for sensitivity analysis is to establish a *base case* or *most likely situation*. Once the base case or most likely forecast elements are established for items such as unit sales, sales price, fixed costs, and variable costs, the analyst will selectively change key variables to determine their impact on the base case results. The analyst can ask all the "what if" questions necessary to see the effect of changes in variables such as product price, raw material costs, and operating costs on the overall results of a project. The analyst can determine which variable has the most negative or positive effect on the project's profitability. Given the possible range of a variable, such as material cost, the range of effects on the outcome can be calculated and evaluated. The more sensitive the outcome is to the tested variable, the more serious an error in estimating the variable would be. The purpose of sensitivity analysis is to identify the variables that have the stronger impact on the outcome of a project. Sensitivity analysis is effective in determining the consequences of a change in a variable.

Sensitivity Analysis: An Example

The following example shows sensitivity analysis as illustrated by break-even analysis. Although break-even analysis has its limitations, it is a useful analytical technique for studying the relationships among fixed costs, variable costs, and revenue. The relationship between costs and revenues must be analyzed to determine at what level of sales total costs are covered by total revenues. Break-even analysis indicates that point at which there is *no* profit or loss. The break-even point serves as a base indication of how many units of product must be sold if a company is to avoid a loss. Figure 5.1 illustrates the break-even concept.

In order to construct a break-even analysis, one must have estimates of fixed costs, variable costs per unit, volume of production, and price per unit. As discussed earlier, fixed costs do not change with the level of production. Variable costs are directly related to units of production and change with the level of production. The following list illustrates different costs attributable to both fixed and variable costs.

Fixed Costs	Variable Costs
Depreciation	Factory labor
Plant equipment	Material costs
Fixed utilities	Commissions
Office expense	Freight in and out
Insurance	Variable factory expense
Rentals	Utilities (other than fixed)
Debt interest	Cost of goods sold
Salaries (executive and office)	Sales expense

The elements and relationships of break-even analysis are illustrated as follows.

Where:

FC	=	Fixed costs
P	=	Sales price per unit
Q	=	Quantity of production in units
V	=	Variable cost per unit
R – V	=	Contribution margin

$$\text{Break-even point} = \frac{\text{Fixed costs}}{\text{Contribution margin}} = \frac{FC}{P - V}$$

Expressed another way:

Total revenue	=	Total cost at the break-even point
TR	=	TC
	or:	
TR – TC	=	0 (at break-even point)
TR	=	PQ = Total revenue
TC	=	FC + VQ = Total cost

Substituting:

$$PQ = FC + VQ$$

Solving for Q will derive break-even quantity.

In a situation where a new production line is being considered, the following data might be indicating by market analysis:

Production line capacity		= 2,200 units		
P	=	Potential selling price	=	$220/unit
FC	=	Fixed costs		= $60,000
V	=	Variable costs		= $170/unit

Figure 5.1 graphically represents the break-even concept. The point at which TR = FC, the break-even point, is 1,200 units.

$$
\begin{aligned}
PQ &= FC + V \times Q \\
\$220\,(Q) &= \$60,000 + \$170\,(Q) \\
\$220\,(Q) - \$170\,(Q) &= \$60,000 \\
\$50\,(Q) &= \$60,000 \\
(Q) &= 1,200 \text{ Units}
\end{aligned}
$$

Solved another way:

$$
\begin{aligned}
\text{Break-even point by quantity} &= \frac{FC}{P - V} \\
&= \frac{\$60,000}{\$220 - \$170} \\
&= \frac{\$60,000}{\$50} \\
&= 1,200
\end{aligned}
$$

With a selling price of $220 per unit, the break-even point is illustrated by the intersection at the lines representing total revenue and total costs in Figure 5.1.

To apply sensitivity analysis, the analyst might put in various values of volume, price, variable cost, and fixed cost to measure their relative effect on profit.

The following list illustrates changes in volume of production of 100 unit increments above and below the break-even point. The list also shows the impact of these changes in production on profits. It shows that changes in the volume of production near the break-even point result in large variations in profits and losses.

Volume	Profit	Percent Change
700	$(25,000)	25%
800	(20,000)	33%
900	(15,000)	50%
1,000	(10,000)	100%
1,100	(5,000)	—
1,200	-0-	—
1,300	5,000	—
1,400	10,000	100%
1,500	15,000	50%
1,600	20,000	33%
1,700	25,000	25%

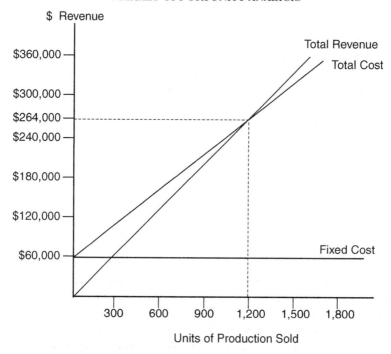

FIGURE 5.1. The break-even concept.

Using the same basic formula previously shown, an analyst can test the sensitivity of price and profits. The following list shows a sensitivity analysis of price and profits (volume set at 1,200 units).

Price	Profit	Percent change
180	(48,000)	33%
190	(36,000)	50%
200	(24,000)	100%
210	(12,000)	—
220	-0-	—
230	12,000	—
240	24,000	100%
250	36,000	50%
260	48,000	33%

Since our example shows a production capacity of 2,200 units and a break-even point of 1,200 units, if market analysis shows a market potential in the range of 1,400 to 1,700 units, then the project can be considered as a very viable proposition. Further calculations can be made to estimate a range of profits based on our previous cost assumptions.

$$\text{Profit} = \$220\,(1,700) - \$60,000 - \$170\,(1,700)$$
$$\text{Profit} = \$374,000 - \$60,000 - \$289,000$$
$$\text{Profit} = \underline{\$25,000}$$

$$\text{Profit} = \$220\,(1,400) - \$60,000 - \$170\,(1,400)$$
$$\text{Profit} = \$308,000 - \$60,000 - \$238,000$$
$$\text{Profit} = \underline{\$10,000}$$

This same information is given on pages 81 and 82.

The analyst can use the same calculation method to compute a minimum sales price for any level of volume. Other variations can be used to determine the effect of changes on profit and loss. Break-even analysis, used in this way, provides managers with a profit or loss estimate at different levels of sales and at different cost estimates. It can also approximate the effect of a change in selling prices on the company.

Sensitivity analysis can be applied to other techniques of analysis as well. It may be used in the capital budgeting decision using discounted cash flows. Changes in the required rate of a return can be quickly converted into changes in the project's net present value, which represents the potential increase in wealth the project offers. The discounted cash flow method of making capital budgeting decisions will be discussed more fully in Chapter 6.

Other uses of sensitivity analysis include testing price change impact on sales plans, testing changes in the productive life of equipment, and testing the changes in demand on profitability.

Risk analysis. Sensitivity analysis is appropriate for asking "what if" questions and for determining the consequences of various changes in relevant variables. Sensitivity analysis, however, cannot identify the likelihood that a change in a variable will occur. Risk analysis is the process used to identify and assign a degree of likelihood to changes in important variables that may be essential in determining the feasibility of a project or venture. This will be discussed in greater detail in Chapter 6.

THE PROCESS OF COST FORECASTING

The use of cost estimates for planning purposes is very important in developing the project cost summary. The firm's chief accounting officer should be instrumental in assembling the cost data used as a basis for a company's new venture activities.

As demand analysis estimated the market potential of the new project, product, or services, cost analysis is the basis for determining the actual financial and technical feasibility of the proposed activity.

Cost estimates must be provided for the following categories.

1. Fixed investments such as land, buildings, fixtures, and other equipment.
2. Manufacturing costs such as direct material cost, direct labor cost, and manufacturing overhead.
3. Start-up expenses such as training costs, increased overtime, scrap expense, consulting fees, and legal fees.
4. Other related expenses.

A broad series of assumptions and decisions must be made to provide the framework for developing these cost estimates. A detailed step-by-step forecasting checklist must be followed to establish accurate cost estimates. An example of this type of checklist is illustrated in Exhibit 5.1.

Accurate cost estimates require a solid analysis of the technical requirements of the projects. Projects will vary in the depth of this type of analysis. The technological complexity of the project, the amount of resources required to accomplish the project, and the number of viable alternatives will influence the amount of attention given to the technical analysis. Most new ventures have enough "unknown" characteristics to require close attention to the specific aspects of the project, in order to achieve good cost estimates.

TECHNICAL ANALYSIS

A large error in the technical study of a project can have significant impact. An inadequate technical study can lead to an immediate failure of the new venture or to costly readjustment of project goals. The

EXHIBIT 5.1. Cost forecast checklist.

	Yes	No
Are the objectives of the study clearly defined?	___	___
Are the various alternatives clearly identified?	___	___
Are reliable cost estimates available for fixed investment, manufacturing costs, and other related start-up costs?	___	___
Are the likely changes in material costs identified?	___	___
Are the likely changes in labor costs identified?	___	___
Are the changes in unit factory overhead rates caused by the proposed production identified?	___	___
Has the demand analysis provided a realistic forecast of sales?	___	___
Have the production personnel provided estimated overhead costs for the new project based on the sales forecast?	___	___
Have all appropriate departments input their budget estimates? (General and Administrative Departments, Warehousing and Distribution, Selling and Advertising, Research and Development, and so forth)	___	___
Has a final project cost summary been completed?	___	___

estimates of manufacturing costs, investment requirements, start-up costs, and other related expenses necessitate an accurate technical study.

The technical study should include the following seven steps.

Step One

	Yes	No
Will the process work? Can the product be produced? Can the service be delivered?	___	___

In some cases, experiments, research, or tests are required to determine if a new product or process is workable.

Step Two

	Yes	No
Are proper inventory estimates made?	____	____

Proper inventory levels are necessary to meet demand requirements and to maintain an even production schedule. The necessary inventory level must be known in order to make the appropriate cost estimates for inventory requirements. Manufacturing firms usually have three types of inventory:

1. *Raw materials.* Raw materials and component parts are influenced by production schedules, anticipated sales, reliability of supply sources, quantity discounts, and price volatility. "Just-in-time" delivery can be established to minimize the levels of raw materials that need to be held on hand.
2. *Work-in-progress.* This type of inventory consists of the partially complete products located in the plant. The level of work-in-progress inventory is affected by the characteristics of the production process, particularly its length. This type of inventory is necessary for a smooth production schedule.
3. *Finished goods.* The level of finished products in stock depends on the right balance between production and sales. A safety stock is necessary to ensure that there is no delay in filling customer orders. Also, finished goods will build up when sales fluctuate and levels of production do not. Inventories of this type are used for production stabilization purposes.

Inventory levels should be estimated to minimize the total cost of ordering inventory and holding inventory. Estimating inventories at approximately 10 percent of the forecasted annual demand provided by the market analysis is a good rule of thumb.

Step Three

	Yes	No
Has the production schedule been developed?	____	____

The projected production requirements are necessary to establish a production schedule. The market analysis should provide estimates of monthly or quarterly sales that can be used for this purpose. After a production schedule has been developed, tangible production cost estimates can be made and prepared for the project cost summary. The cost of the production process must include all the sequence of operations and functions required to convert raw material inventory into finished goods inventory. This should include the cost of

- production equipment
- handling equipment (conveyors, hoists, cranes, and so forth)
- space requirements
- inventory levels
- personnel (production and supervision)
- delivery
- inspection
- maintenance

Step three leads, out of necessity, directly into steps four, five, and six.

Step Four

	Yes	No
Are special tools and equipment necessary?	___	___

If the answer is "yes," steps must be taken to analyze the costs related to these necessary items. Cost information concerning special tools and equipment can be obtained from:

- equipment manufacturers
- trade literature
- other manufacturers using the same or similar equipment
- trade associations

In some cases, a capital budgeting analysis of equipment alternatives is necessary. Since present costs cannot be compared dollar for dollar with future costs, an equivalent annual cost in present value terms should be used to choose among alternatives. The present value method of discounting future cost amounts will be discussed and illustrated in Chapter 6.

Step Five

	Yes	No
Have labor requirements and costs been established?	____	____

Accurate cost estimates require the knowledge of how any employees are required and the rates at which the various skill levels must be paid. This information can be used to determine final labor costs. Total workload requirements are estimated for each skill level classification. These totals are then multiplied by the appropriate pay rate that is paid that skill level. In addition to direct production labor, factory overhead must be included. Typical types of factory overhead include

- maintenance
- inspection
- supervision
- receiving
- packing
- shipping
- control
- analysis
- safety
- quality control

Step Six

	Yes	No
Have the various space requirements and costs been established?	____	____

Most projects will require various types of space considerations. Most common are:

- production space
- sales space
- administrative space
- other service space

Production space includes work areas, storage areas, and testing areas. Layout charts and process charts can be helpful in calculating the actual square footage of space required.

Other space requirements should be reasonably estimated in order to calculate building or rental costs. These other areas include

- administrative offices
- meeting rooms
- sales areas
- training rooms
- accounting and auditing areas
- safety office
- security office
- breakrooms (showers, lunch area, etc.)
- research and development area
- purchasing area
- quality control
- engineering
- maintenance
- warehouse space
- toolroom
- personnel offices

If the project requires the decision to build a building, then that aspect of the project should be approached as a feasibility project within the larger opportunity assessment project. The same basic steps should be followed to examine the market factors, the cost factors, and the financial consideration of a new site location.

Step Seven

	Yes	No
Has the project cost summary been completed?	___	___

The cost estimates obtained through the other steps in this process are important in defining the financial nature of an opportunity. The integrity of the financial analysis and the estimated return on investment depends on the accuracy of the demand analysis (sales estimates) and the cost analysis (cost estimates). These analyses should provide the parameters to determine ROI.

The project cost summary must include the basic cost elements mentioned at the beginning of the forecasting portion of this chapter. They are:

1. Fixed investment
2. Manufacturing cost
3. Start-up costs
4. Other related costs

Exhibit 5.2 illustrates a project cost summary including the four basic cost elements. The project cost summary provides the information necessary for a projected statement of the cost of goods sold. This, coupled with information from the market analysis, provides the basis for the pro forma income statement. This estimates the profitability of the project. Pro forma income statements are exhibited in Appendix B. Additional aids can now be produced to assist the planner such as pro forma balance sheets, cash flow projections, and detailed cost summaries.

PROCEDURES

Forecasting Procedures

Cost forecasting can utilize many of the tools described in Chapter 2 in relation to forecasting sales. Developing cost forecasts of totally new ventures for which there is no historical cost figures is more difficult and subject to greater error than forecasts for projects that have cost histories.

The correct procedure to forecast costs varies from project to project. The objective of cost forecasting is to approximate the real expenses involved in an undertaking so profitability can be projected. The actual procedure for forecasting cost may be determined by an examination of the objectives and resources of the principals to the venture.

EXHIBIT 5.2. Project cost summary.

Category	Quantity	Description	Costs Monthly	Annual
Fixed Investment		Land	____	____
		Construction cost	____	____
		Building cost	____	____
		Security systems	____	____
		Fire prevention system	____	____
		Furniture	____	____
		Fixtures	____	____
		Production equipment	____	____
		Office equipment	____	____
		Trucks	____	____
		Other investment	____	____
Manufacturing Costs		Direct material	____	____
		Direct labor	____	____
		Factory overhead	____	____
		Maintenance	____	____
		Utilities	____	____
		Quality control	____	____
		Office supplies	____	____
		Rent	____	____
		Insurance	____	____
		Telephone	____	____
		Depreciation	____	____
		Taxes	____	____
		Supervision	____	____
		Toolroom	____	____
		Misc. expenses	____	____
Start-Up Costs		Financing expense	____	____
		Consultant's fees	____	____
		Training	____	____
		Waste	____	____
		Delay expense	____	____
		Travel	____	____
		Legal fees	____	____

(continued)

(continued)

Other Related Requirements	Patents	___	___
	Other start-up costs	___	___
	Working capital required	___	___
	Extraordinary expenses	___	___
	Administrative expenses	___	___
	Salaries	___	___
	Insurance	___	___
	Supplies	___	___
	Other costs	___	___
	Total Cost	___	___

The following forecasting techniques can be used to estimate costs.

1. *Judgment techniques:* The various experiences of key personnel have led to "rules of thumb" that can, in some cases, determine certain types of costs. These techniques are subjective in nature and should not be the sole basis for cost analysis.

2. *Survey techniques:* Just as market information can be acquired through consumer surveys, so can cost information. Personal or telephone interviews with persons with experience in the appropriate field are commonly used. Such surveys of expert opinion can generate helpful cost data.

3. *Historical data techniques:* When historical data is available, cost forecasting can be accomplished by making certain subjective assumptions and then projecting historical cost elements into the future.

   a. *Trend analysis:* Computer and calculator programs to allow the forecaster to project past points of costs to specific future dates. A simple technique of plotting the past cost history of a certain cost element can be helpful. The scatter diagram technique charts cost data for a number of periods (see Figure 5.2). A line is drawn midway between high and low points. This line is called the line of best fit or the regression line. Remember, many costs are distinct entities and cannot be projected in the same way sales can.

   b. *Multiple regression:* Multiple regression is a more sophisticated approach to forecasting. In simple regression, a cost is assumed to be the function of only one variable. In multiple regression, the cost or dependent variable is dependent on a number of variables.

4. *Percent of sales:* Many costs can be adequately expressed in a percent of sales format. Sales commissions, for example, are calculated as a percentage of sales. A good sales forecast is an essential foundation for this method of estimating costs. The percent of sales method implies a linear relationship between sales and the expense item being calculated. Not only can certain expense items be forecast as a percentage of sales, but balance sheet items and external financing requirements can be developed by this method as well. Table 5.3 illustrates some important costs expressed as a percent of sales.

FIGURE 5.2. Scatter diagram.

TABLE 5.3. Variable cost as a percent of sales.

Cost Category	Fixed Cost	Variable Cost	Variable Cost As a Percent of Sales (Sales = $70,000)
Raw materials	—	$3,100	4.4%
Direct labor	—	27,500	39.3
Indirect labor	200	150	0.2
Factory maintenance	100	100	0.1
Utilities	500	400	0.6
Property tax	300	—	—
Depreciation	900	—	—
Sales commissions	—	5,250	7.5
Advertising	—	1,200	1.7
Sales expense	2,200	800	1.1
Administrative salaries	25,000	—	—
Depreciation (Office)	750	—	—
Bad debt expense	1,200	—	—
Totals	$31,150	$38,500	55.0%

SUMMARY

Accurately estimating the financial impact of a decision is extremely difficult. Unknowns and contingencies can cause forecasts to vary from actual revenues. Nonetheless, the revenue forecast is a basic prerequisite to complete financial analysis. Overly optimistic forecasts produce unrealistic expectations, whereas overly pessimistic predictions may lead a firm to pass up a good opportunity.

Accurate cost estimation is extremely important to opportunity assessment also. Cost overruns are common and often disastrous to the principals involved in a venture. Consequently, every attempt should be made to *identify* and *estimate* accurately all costs associated with a specific opportunity. This is best accomplished by a thorough technical study and an accompanying cost forecast. The results of the forecasting process should yield a project cost summary that can be used in determining ROIs, which is discussed in Chapter 6.

Chapter 6

Profitability Analysis

The final and perhaps overriding consideration in defining the exact nature of an opportunity is the potential profitability it represents. Previous chapters have dealt with the analysis of demand and the forecasting of costs associated with assessing market and business opportunities. This chapter will focus on the analytical techniques which can be used to ensure profitable investment decisions.

One of the major objectives of all the time, energy, and resources marshaled toward a project is to generate a "good" profit. What is a "good" profit, however, may be a matter of personal judgment. However, it is advisable to establish certain acceptable levels of ROI before choosing a project alternative.

RETURN ON INVESTMENT

Simply stated, return on investment (ROI) is how much the investment returns to you on an annual basis. ROI is the most meaningful and popular measure of economic success. The term is widely understood by accountants, financial analysts, bankers, managers, and investors. ROI analysis is very helpful in determining the health of a project. ROI itself, however, does not measure the safety of an investment, only its performance expressed as a percentage.

Return on investment can be calculated by dividing net profit by the total investment required to generate the profit. The following formula illustrates the calculation of ROI:

$$\text{ROI} = \frac{\text{Net profit}}{\text{Total investment}}$$

$$\text{ROI} = 21.5\% = \frac{\$42,000}{\$195,000}$$

ROI can be calculated for a wide range of investments including savings accounts, profit centers, divisions, and entire companies. ROI can also be expressed as a combination of the profit margin on sales and the turnover activity ratio of an investment.

Net profits divided by sales equals the profit margin.

$$\frac{\text{Net profit}}{\text{Sales}} = \text{Pr ofit margin}$$

Sales divided by investment = Turnover of assets

$$\frac{\text{Sales}}{\text{Investment}} = \text{Turnover}$$

Return on investment is equal to Turnover × Profit Margin

$$\frac{\text{Net profit}}{\text{Sales}} \times \frac{\text{Sales}}{\text{Investment}} = \text{ROI}$$

This second approach to determining ROI brings together the profitability margin on sales and the activity ratio of asset (investment) turnover. This approach takes into consideration the combination of the efficient use of assets (investments) and the profit margin on sales. This method, the Du Pont system of financial analysis, has been widely accepted in American industry.

FINANCIAL ANALYSIS PROCESS

Financial analysis and capital budgeting consist of the process of selecting among alternative investments in land, buildings, productive equipment, or other assets for future gain. Since decisions of this type usually commit the firm to a long-term course of action, careful analysis is required to identify the potential return.

Capital budgeting is theoretically very simple. List all the investment opportunities available, rank them according to profitability, and accept all investments up to the point at which marginal benefits equal marginal cost. However, in reality the complexity of revolving planning horizons makes the choice of capital outlays more difficult. Different project length, start-up time, and payout time make meaningful comparisons among investment alternatives problematic.

The depth of the economic analysis needed depends on the type of project, its urgency, and the objectives of the firm. For example, a burned-out generator in a power plant must be replaced. The decision is not replacement versus nonreplacement; the decision concerns only which particular generator is most productive, least costly, or most readily available.

DECISION FLOW CHART

Before detailing the analytical techniques for determining profitability and for making capital decisions, a framework for the decision process—a decision flow chart—should be established.

Step One: Problem Definition

The first step appears obvious; however, it is often overlooked. Often a statement of a problem (e.g., "The problem is we need more trucks") is not a problem statement at all but, rather, a suggested alternative solution. Too often decision makers jump prematurely to step two without clearly articulating the problem. The importance of proper problem definition cannot be overemphasized. Replacement of a worn-out piece of equipment, development of a new product, and the construction of a new plant all create uniquely complex problems to overcome. Each of these examples generally produces several alternatives, which must be identified and evaluated clearly.

Step Two: Identify Alternatives

Alternative actions can range from doing nothing, going out of business, replacing with the same type of equipment, replacing with different equipment, replacing with larger or smaller equipment, and so on. From this wide range of alternatives, only the appropriate alternatives should be selected for further analysis.

Step Three: Identify Relevant Costs and Revenues

The next step is to identify the relevant costs and revenues that will change as a result of the action taken. Chapter 3 dealt with many aspects of technical analysis and cost forecasting that also apply to this step in the capital budgeting process. Do not assume that past operating costs will apply to new ventures. Although it is tempting simply to project historical cost into the future, it is very hazardous to do so. Methods of dealing with the uncertainty surrounding the cost and revenue flows involved in capital budgeting must be incorporated to identify and estimate costs of revenues realistically.

The basic question asked in step three is, "What are the changes in costs and revenues that will occur because of an action taken?" Other questions to be addressed include

- What additional revenues will be generated?
- What revenues will be lost?
- What is the net impact of the action on revenue?
- What additional costs will be generated?
- What costs will be eliminated?
- What is the net impact of the action on costs?

These questions lead to the economic principle of incremental changes in cash flow. The focus is on the economic cash flow concept. Once an after-tax cash flow change has been determined, we are ready for step four.

Step Four: Determine the Alternative with the Most Beneficial Result

The capital budgeting decision alternative with the most positive return on investment is generally considered the superior one. The specific method of analysis used to calculate which alternative has the most sufficient economic returns over the life of the investment must in some way take into account the trade-off of current cash outlay and future cash inflow.

THE METHODS OF ANALYZING INVESTMENTS

Many methods are available to evaluate investment alternatives prior to making the capital budgeting decision. Some of the more common methods will be discussed here.

The focus of capital budgeting is to make decisions that maximize the value of a firm's investment. We must choose a method that will answer most appropriately the question, "Which is the most profitable alternative?" The most common criteria for choosing among alternatives may be identified as non–time value methods and time value methods.

1. Non–time value methods
    a. Payback period
    b. Simple ROI
    c. Average ROI
2. Time value methods
    a. Net present value
    b. Internal rate of return
    c. Present value index

Each of these methods has its advantages and disadvantages which will be discussed along with the description of each method.

Payback Period

The payback period method is simply an estimate of how long it will take for the investment to pay for itself. No interest factors are included in the calculations. Once the payback period is determined, it is usually compared with a rule of thumb or standard period. If the investment is determined to pay for itself in less time than the standard period, the investment would be made. In deciding between mutually exclusive alternatives, the one with the shortest payback period is generally chosen.

The payback period can be calculated in several ways. The most common one uses the formula:

$$\text{Payback} = \frac{\text{Net investment outlay}}{\text{Net annual cash flow benefits}}$$

When annual cash flow benefits are irregular or investment outlay comes in various time frames, Table 6.1 can be used to determine the payback period. In this case the payback period is four years.

The payback period method is widely used because of its ease of calculation. Because it does not take into consideration the time value of money, however, it has serious flaws of logic.

Advantages

1. The calculations are easy.
2. Choosing the project with shortest payback period has the more favorable short-run effect on earnings per share.
3. The method is easily understood.

Disadvantages

1. The method completely ignores all cash flows beyond the payback period.
2. Does not adjust for risk related to uncertainty.
3. Ignores the time value of money.

Some firms are beginning to use the payback method in combination with one or more of the time value methods described next. When this is done, the payback method is used as a risk measurement, and the time value method is used as an indicator of profitability.

TABLE 6.1. Determination of payback period.

Year	Investment Outlay	Annual Cash Flow Benefits	Cumulative Cash Flow
1	$150,000	$40,000	($110,000)
2	10,000	40,000	(80,000)
3	0	40,000	(40,000)
4	0	40,000	0
5	0	40,000	40,000
6	0	20,000	60,000
7	0	20,000	80,000

Simple ROI

The simple ROI method is an outgrowth of the logic of the payback method. This method can be represented by manipulating the payback formula. Simple ROI is an attempt to express the desirability of an investment in terms of a percentage return on the original investment outlay.

$$\text{ROI} = \frac{\text{Net annual cash flow benefits}}{\text{Net investment outlay}}$$

The simple ROI method has all the drawbacks and disadvantages of the payback method. No reference at all is made to the project's economic life. An investment of $40,000 with an average annual benefit of $8,000 will yield a 20 percent return regardless of whether the length of the project is one, five, or ten years.

$$\text{ROI} = \frac{\$8,000}{\$40,000}$$

Average ROI

The expected average rate of ROI of the estimated profitability of an investment. This calculation differs from the simple ROI by employing the average net investment.

$$\text{Average ROI} = \frac{\text{Net annual cash flow benefits}}{\text{Average net investment outlay}}$$

Assuming straight-line depreciation and no residual value at the end of its life, an average investment would be equal to 50 percent of the original investment. Using the previous example, a net annual cash flow of $8,000 on an original expenditure of $40,000 would be 40 percent, not 20 percent.

$$\text{Average ROI} = \frac{\$8,000}{\$20,000} = 40\%$$

Advanced Concepts of Analysis: Time Value Methods

Investment decision values involve the trade-off between current dollar outlays and future benefits over a period of time. As a result, it is not prudent to ignore the timing of the benefits of investment alternatives. In this regard, the quicker the return the better. Money has value directly related to the timing of its receipt or disbursement. The delay of receiving money means an opportunity cost in terms of lost income. Thus, it is obviously preferable to receive benefits quickly and defer expenditures.

Net Present Value Method

The basic idea of the net present value (NPV) method is to overcome the disadvantage of non–time value methods. The NPV method provides a balance or trade-off between investment outlays and future benefits in terms of time-adjusted dollars. The present value (PV) of discounted cash flows is an amount that is equivalent to a project's cash flow for a particular interest rate. Generally, the interest rate used to discount future cash flows is a company's cost of capital rate. The NPV method involves

1. Determining the PV of the net investment cost outlay.
2. Estimating the future cash flow benefits.
3. Discounting the future cash flows to present value at the appropriate cost of capital.
4. Subtracting the present value of the costs from the PV of the benefits.

If the amount derived from step four is positive, then the investment is considered to be a profitable investment since the time adjusted internal rate of return of the investment is greater than the cost of capital. Conversely, a negative figure indicates that the project is earning a rate of return less than the cost of capital chosen by the firm as a standard of decision.

NPV can be calculated by the following formula:

$$NPV = \frac{R_1}{(1+i)^1} + \frac{R_2}{(1+i)^2} + \frac{R_3}{(1+i)^n} - IC$$

Where:

NPV = Net present value of the investment
  R = Expected dollar return or cash flow each year
  i = Appropriate interest rate (cost of capital)
  IC = Present value of the investment cost
  n = Project's expected life

The NPVs of two alternative projects are illustrated in Table 6.2. Project 1 has the highest return, even though the payback period is identical. The greatest benefit will be provided by selecting the alternative. If the two projects are not mutually exclusive and funds are available, both investment opportunities should be accepted.

This method has several advantages which make it more suitable than the payback methods as a basis of comparing investments.

TABLE 6.2. Net present values.

Year	Net Return or Cash Flow		Interest Factor $(1 + i)_n$	PV of Cash Flow	
Project 1					
1	$400	×	0.91	$364	
2	500	×	0.83	415	
3	600	×	0.75	450	
4	800	×	0.68	544	
				1,773	PV of inflows
				−1,500	Less PV of cost
				$273	NPV
Project 2					
1	800	×	0.91	$728	
2	300	×	0.83	249	
3	400	×	0.75	300	
4	400	×	0.68	272	
				1,549	PV of inflows
				−1,500	Less PV of cost
				$49	NPV

Advantages

1. Considers the time value of money.
2. Concentrates the values of costs and benefits in a comparable time frame.
3. The method is fairly simple to understand and calculate.

Disadvantages

1. Assumes benefits and costs can be estimated for the lifetime of the project.
2. Requires equal time periods for comparison of several investment alternatives.
3. The method is sensitive to changes in the interest rate used to discount the values.

Internal Rate of Return

The internal rate of return (IRR) is simply the yield of a project. The IRR is defined as the interest rate that discounts the future cash flows, or receipts, and makes them equal to the initial cost outlay. The time value of money is taken into consideration. The formula used for NPV can also be used for calculating the IRR with one slight variation. Instead of solving for NPV, the PV of the cost is made equal to the PV of the benefits. The equation is solved for the interest rate that will make the PV of the cost equal to the PV of the benefits. In other words, the IRR of a project is the discount interest rate that generates a net present value of zero. Below is the NPV formula and the change necessary to create the IRR formula.

NPV Formula

$$NPV = \frac{R_1}{(1+i)^1} + \frac{R_2}{(1+i)^2} + K + \frac{R_n}{(1+i)^n} - IC$$

IRR Formula

$$IRR = \frac{R_1}{(1+i)^1} + \frac{R_2}{(1+i)^2} + K + \frac{R_n}{(1+i)^n} - IC$$

or

$$O = \frac{R_1}{(1+i)^1} + \frac{R_2}{(1+i)^2} + K + \frac{R_n}{(1+i)^n} - IC$$

Solve for i and $i = IRR$.

In the formula for IRR, i represents the interest rate that equates the present values of the benefits and the costs of a project. In the NPV formula, i represents the firm's cost of capital. When the cost of capital is used in the formula and $NPV = 0$, then the internal rate of return is equal to the cost of capital. When NPV is positive, the IRR is greater than the cost of capital. When NPV is negative, the IRR is less than the cost of capital. Whenever the IRR is greater than the firm's cost of capital, the investment is a positive one. The IRR can be found by trial and error. The IRR method is widely accepted as a ranking device. The yield is reasonably accurate and much superior to the simple payback and simple return on investment methods.

Advantages

1. Because the IRR method is closely related to the NPV method, it is familiar to many business practitioners and thus more readily accepted.
2. Calculation of the firm's cost of capital is not required as it is with the NPV method.
3. The method time-values money.

Disadvantages

1. The IRR does not do a good job of comparing investments having large differences in magnitude. For example, a $20,000 investment with an IRR of 42 percent cannot be compared with an investment of $100,000 with an IRR of 30 percent. It may be far better to marshal all resources toward the $100,000 investment even though the IRR is lower than the other investment.
2. In the same manner, length of the life of the investment is also important. It may be more advantageous to invest funds at a lower IRR for a longer term than to invest short-term for a slightly higher IRR. The pertinent criticism of the IRR method

is that it assumes reinvestment can be made at the IRR, which may not be true.

Present Value Index

This method is similar to the present value method. A ratio is determined between the present value of the cash flow benefits and the present values of the net investment outlays. The present value index (PVI) is sometimes referred to as the benefit/cost ratio of discounted cash flows. Several alternative projects may have similar NPVs but require widely different investment amounts. To choose an alternative simply on the size of NPV would ignore the relative different sizes of the projects. Equal NPVs coming from different size investments will have different IRRs. A formal way of expressing this difference is to compare the projects on a benefits/costs basis.

$$PVI = \frac{\text{Present value of cash flow benefits}}{\text{Present value of net investment outlay}}$$

The higher the index, the better the project. However, any PVI over 1.0 beats the minimum standard built into the calculation of PV and should be funded. Most projects, however, are competing for limited funds.

Table 6.3 includes examples of the PVI. A comparison is made of the PVI and the NPV ranking methods. Slightly different results are given. Notice that alternatives 1 and 3 have the same NPV, but alternative 1 has the higher PVI and is, therefore, more favorable.

The advantages and disadvantages of the PVI method are similar to those listed for the NPV method.

TABLE 6.3. Present value index.

Alternative	PV of Benefits	PV of Costs	NPV	PVI
1	$10,500	$8,500	$2,000	1.24
2	16,000	13,000	3,000	1.23
3	15,000	13,000	2,000	1.15
4	17,500	18,500	−1,000	.95
5	20,000	16,000	4,000	1.25

RISK ANALYSIS

The classical definition of the riskiness of an asset is the probability that the future returns expected will fall below expected levels. This is often measured by the standard deviation or the coefficient of variation of expected returns. In the earlier discussion of the various methods of making capital budget decisions, the only treatment for risk was the informal aspect of making judgments concerning estimates at economic life and cash flow amounts. Some situations, however, call for a more formal assessment of risk and the effect of uncertainty. We referred to sensitivity analysis in Chapter 5. Sensitivity analysis can be used to calculate a project's NPVs under alternative assumptions to see how sensitive NPV is to changing circumstances.

Projects for which the variability in expected returns is very large require an even more formal approach to evaluating risk. Risk analysis attempts to identify the likelihood that events will occur. Risk results from lack of experience, misinterpretation of data, bias in forecasting, errors in analysis, and changes in economic conditions. In the process of project feasibility analysis and assessment, a number of variables are usually in question.

More than seven out of ten surveyed companies report that they employ some type of risk analysis in project analysis. Some of the most common risk evaluaton techniques are: risk-adjusted discount rate or rate of return, risk-adjusted cash flows, and risk-adjusted payback periods.

Risk-Adjusted Discount Rate

One of the most frequently used methods is the risk-adjusted discount rate method. The basic objective of this method is to increase the applied discount rate when dealing with risky projects. (If the simple rate of return method is being used, the cutoff rate is raised to allow for a greater "cushion" for risky projects.) The increase in the discount rate (cost of capital) is a risk premium to protect the firm from uncertainty of future cash flows of uncertain investments.

As mentioned earlier, the variability of the probability distributions of expected returns can be estimated. In some cases, it can be estimated objectively with statistical techniques. In many situations, the estimates must be determined by subjective probability distributions.

Once the probability distribution has been determined, the variability of the distribution can be measured using standard deviation or coefficient of variation. The project with the larger deviation represents the greatest risk and is assigned the higher discount rate.

The higher discount rate reduces the PV of the future benefits and makes it more difficult for a risky investment to achieve a positive NPV. Consequently, marginal projects that are more risky will be rejected.

The risk-adjusted discount rate method is easy to apply but it has some disadvantages. Usually the adjusted rate applies to all costs and revenues, even ones that can be estimated with relative certainty. The lack of discrimination among the cost and revenue estimates is the major criticism of this method.

Risk-Adjusted Cash Flows

As forecasts are made to develop the point estimate or most likely estimate, the analyst will incorporate into the estimate the risk he perceives. He or she then defines the degree of uncertainty in terms of probability of occurrence. For example, an "optimistic," "most likely," and "pessimistic" estimate is made taking historical data, environmental analysis, and expected trends into consideration. This three-level method of forecasting was exhibited in Chapter 2.

To illustrate, consider the following calculation of the expected value of cash flows from two projects.

Project 1 *Cash Flow*	*Project 2* *Cash Flow*	*State of Economy* *(Probability)*
850	350	.2 Recession
700	900	.5 Normal
400	500	.3 Boom
		1.0

Table 6.4 shows the calculation of expected value based on the data shown in this list.

The expected value of the cash flow of project 1 is $640 instead of the $700 point estimate, while the expected value of the cash flows of project 2 is $670 rather than $900. The expected value gives the forecaster and decision maker a better feeling for the risk involved in the decision.

TABLE 6.4. Expected value of cash flow.

Cash Flow	Probability of Economic Condition	Expected Value
Project 1		
$850	.2 Recession	$170
700	.5 Normal	350
400	.3 Boom	120
	1.0	$640
Project 2		
$350	.2 Recession	$70
900	.5 Normal	450
500	.3 Boom	150
	1.0	$670

The risk-adjusted cash flow is generally lower than the best-estimate cash flow. The effect of using a risk-adjusted cash flow in the NPV method of capital budgeting is a lower NPV than would have been obtained by using the best estimate cash flow. The result is that marginal projects with risky potential benefit are more readily discarded.

Simulation Models

Computer simulation can be used to extend probability concepts in decision making. The use of the computer allows for decision makers to estimate, for each of a dozen or so variables of major products, ranges of possible outcomes and the probability distributions for these ranges. The focus might be placed on sales volume, prices, key cost elements, salvage values, interest rate fluctuations, or cash flows. A series of outcomes of the project is then developed by the computer simulation. The computer output will allow statements to be made, such as: "There is a 65 percent likelihood that the net present value of the project will be $200,000" or "There is a one-in-ten chance that the project will lose $210,000." The sophistication of this type of analysis and the vast number of variables places obvious limitations on its use.

COST ANALYSIS FOR NOT-FOR-PROFIT ENTITIES

The concept of "not-for-profit entities" is a broadening one, including many different types of economic structures such as churches, government organizations, universities, hospitals, charitable institutions, clubs, fraternal groups, and cooperatives. Income, the traditional measure of success for a profit entity, is less of a measure of efficiency for an organization that does not intend to make profits. Thus traditional break-even analysis is a difficult concept to apply to not-for-profit entities (see Chapter 5).

Projects of any economic organization should be evaluated for their ability to meet the objectives of the organization within the budget constraints and incomes generated by the activity. With not-for-profit entities this is complicated by the fact that their services cannot always be expressed in dollar terms.

Benefit/Cost Analysis

Cost analysis for not-for-profit organizations is difficult because some costs are difficult to assign. When a nonprofit organization is choosing between alternative programs that fall within the scope of their objectives, benefit/cost analysis can be helpful. Benefit/cost analysis is a formalized attempt to obtain the maximum benefits from a given level of funding. A community wants the best possible police protection, a university wants the best faculty, and the Red Cross wants the most effective blood donor recruiting program that the given level of funding can support. Benefit/cost analysis allows a nonprofit organization to evaluate various alternatives.

Each program can be evaluated based on a comparison of benefit/cost ratios. For example, a public library may be considering the addition of a new business section, a film rental library, or an arts library. These alternatives are exhibited in the following list.

Alternative	Benefits	Costs	Net Benefit	B/C Ratio
1	$32,500	$28,400	$4,100	1.14
2	48,000	40,000	8,000	1.20
3	17,700	22,800	–5,100	.78

Alternatives 1 and 2 have a positive net benefit, and a benefit/cost ratio greater than one. Alternative 2 has the most favorable benefit/cost ratio. However, if the library has approximately $80,000 available, it should embark on both alternatives. Alternative 3 fails both the net benefit test and the benefit/cost ratio test. Unless there are other overriding nonfinancial considerations, alternative 3 should be rejected. The basic disadvantage of this type of analysis is the difficulty of estimating both costs and benefits. Costs are perhaps the easiest part of the equation. Cost of construction, equipment, supplies, salaries, and so forth, can usually be accurately estimated. Social costs are more difficult to appraise. On the other hand, benefit analysis poses many difficult problems. As we attempt to identify each type of benefit, we run into some social, aesthetic, and nonmonetary benefits. How these are assigned dollar values radically influences the benefit/cost analysis.

Cost-Effectiveness Analysis

When there is difficulty comparing alternatives on the benefit/cost basis, cost effectiveness analysis may be appropriate. Cost effectiveness analysis deals with the effect of variations in cost on benefit. The focus of this analysis is to determine effectiveness of operations rather than trying to see how much more benefit there is than cost.

SUMMARY

This chapter has dealt with the process and methods of making capital budgeting decisions. The final consideration of the overall financial analysis is, "How profitable will the project be?" The concept of ROI is essential to answering this question. The analysis should lead to a clear "yes" or "no." In some cases, however, an "I don't know" will be the response.

To answer the question "yes" implies that the market exists, costs are identifiable and controllable, the process or service works, the financial ROI are satisfactory and the uncertainty is tolerable. In other words, the overall opportunity assessment has determined that the project is both feasible and profitable.

Chapter 7 will show how to bring these financial considerations into focus with a firm's own purpose and resources. This leads to a climax of the process—a decision about whether the opportunity should be pursued.

PART IV:
INTERNAL ANALYSIS

Chapter 7

Feasibility Analysis:
Summary and Action Plan

The analysis described thus far enters the decision-making realm in this chapter. The decision maker at this stage must decide which, if any, of the market opportunities represent company opportunities (i.e., opportunities the company should pursue).

Special attention is given to the factors which must be analyzed in assessing opportunities and the tools needed for the analysis. A special summary worksheet is provided to assimilate the essential facts from the previous analysis as individual opportunities are analyzed.

PROBLEMS VERSUS OPPORTUNITIES

Problems and opportunities must be differentiated, although some of the same types of analysis are appropriate for dealing with either situation. A problem is defined as anything that stands in the way of reaching an objective, whereas an opportunity is a chance to improve an overall performance. To be experiencing a problem, a firm must have already identified objectives it wants to accomplish and have tried to accomplish them. The failure of performance to meet expectations spelled out in a statement of objectives is by definition a problem. Assuming that realistic objectives have been established the planner must (1) define the exact nature of the problem, (2) identify alternative courses of action (strategies), and (3) select a course of action (strategy) to solve that problem. For the analyst dealing with existing problems, resources have already been committed, and decisions revolve around continuing the commitment, the extent of additional commitments and the nature of the commitments. The analyst dealing with opportunities is in a somewhat different position. Either the company has not been involved in the market prior to the analysis or it is not experiencing a failure to reach objectives, but is instead searching for new markets to enter or ways to improve on current performance.

One of the basic differences in opportunity analysis is that it involves alignment of market opportunities with purpose and resources, and in many cases, goes beyond the realm of a functional decision because it involves a new commitment of resources. It may be, in fact, that the types of analysis described thus far are the basic inputs into a capital budgeting decision, which is beyond the scope of the analyst's job description.

To successfully evaluate opportunities, the analyst must combine the external and financial analysis with internal analysis, which directly influences a firm's willingness and ability to respond to opportunities. The internal factors include purpose or mission and company resources.

INTERNAL FACTORS

Purpose

The presence of marketing opportunities is a necessary condition for action, but it is not sufficient by itself. Management must decide if it wants to take advantage of the existing opportunity and whether it has the resources to exploit a given opportunity successfully. That is, it must decide if the opportunity in the marketplace represents a company opportunity. There are always opportunities available, but not all companies are equally prepared to handle them. The purpose of the organization has a select bearing on which market opportunities are pursued (as was pointed out in Chapter 2 in discussing the impact of purpose on company opportunities). A company's statement of purpose or mission should be used to evaluate market opportunities. Market activities and purpose must align. The organization wants to pursue only those ventures which will help fulfill its overall mission and reject those which do not.

If, for example, a company mission is defined as a developer of high-quality paints, the identification of a market segment which needs a low-quality paint product in large quantities should not be viewed as a company opportunity regardless of how attractive that segment appears in terms of market potential and lack of competition. Trying to serve the needs of such a segment is in direct opposition to what the company has stated as its mission and must be rejected if the statement of mission is to be retained.

Company Resources

Given that an opportunity is consistent with purpose, the resources of the firm must be analyzed to determine the company's ability to respond to an opportunity. At least four types of resources must be analyzed.

Marketing Resources

A firm's ability to take advantage of opportunities requires personnel with the marketing skills necessary to develop and execute effective marketing strategies. A good product does not insure success. The old adage of "build a better mousetrap and the world will beat a path to your door" is just not true. Good marketing is the result of good marketers. Many firms who were successful in the industrial market have failed in the consumer market because of a lack of know-how in dealing with those markets. If a firm does not have adequate marketing skills available within its own organization, the company's financial resources must be sufficient to acquire the marketing personnel or it must look for acquisition of a successful firm already positioned in the market who has strong marketing abilities.

An example of the influence of marketing resources on a firm's success is illustrated by a large chemical company's experience with a new consumer product. This company has been a leader in manufacturing and marketing chemical products aimed at the industrial market for years. Several years ago the company developed a new cleaning compound and decided to sell it in the consumer market. The company was unsuccessful in its attempt because of a lack of experience in marketing consumer products. This product was sold to a consumer-goods firm that successfully marketed the product. Thus it was inexperience in marketing consumer goods that caused the company's lack of success, not the absence of an opportunity.

Physical Resources

Two distinctly difficult physical response elements affect the firm's ability to handle new opportunities—*productive capability* and *technological agility*. The actual capacity for production is influenced by previous commitments to acquire plant and equipment. In the short run this is usually fixed, but it can be altered over time for new strategic opportunities. The technology available during the short run is also considered fixed, and therefore a firm currently must have both the capacity and technology or the ability to contract with firms that do. A watch manufacturer with capacity may not be able to enter the electronic watch market because of the firm's current pin lever watch technology. Unless component parts are subcontracted for, this market opportunity could not be exploited by the firm until new technology is acquired. Financial resources would also be an enabling factor in that situation.

The importance of productive resources is illustrated by the watch industry. The industry was built around pin lever watch technology. Bulova departed from this technology and developed its Accutron watch with a tuning fork. This was the first of a rash of technological changes, including, of course, the electronic watch. As technology developed the price of the electronic watch declined and new competitive forces were at work in the industry.

Many firms were unable to enter the competitive electronic watch market because they did not have the productive technology needed. Also, other firms were able to break into a new market because of their production technology and capacity in electronic components.

Financial Resources

The total amount of financial resources a firm has available and the process through which these funds are allocated influence the firm's ability to enter a market effectively. In some industries there are financial barriers which are insurmountable except for the very largest companies—automobile manufacturers, for example. Not only are productive resources capital intensive but also marketing expenditures are at a high level. Also, although some opportunities appear attractive, the hurdle rate used in the capital budgeting process may be too high. Adequate financial sources must be available to underwrite both production and marketing activities or the firm must have easy access to financial markets before some opportunities can be undertaken.

The absence of financial resources has been the downfall of many companies which had both the production and the marketing resources to be successful. A well-known example is W. T. Grant's department stores. This national chain of department stores closed due to overextended consumer credit. Grant's simply did not have the financial resources to absorb the bad debt losses and were forced into bankruptcy.

Adequate financial resources enabled Southwest Airlines to operate in the Dallas-Houston-San Antonio markets for the first two years while building up enough patronage to sustain a profitable operation. The low sales revenue and high operating costs during the first two years were anticipated, and the financial revenues permitted continued operation. Thus a firm's current financial position plus its ability to successfully enter capital markets directly influences its ability to pursue opportunities.

Managerial Resources

The other important part of the resource base which must be analyzed is managerial resources. This was referred to earlier in terms of matching skills. Management willingness to take risk, their values, skills, age, and experience are all important aspects reflecting an organization's ability to respond to opportunities.

Financial resources can be used to offset managerial shortcomings through hiring new managers for opportunities which represent a distinct departure from current operations. This was pointed out in Chapter 2 when conglomerate diversification was discussed.

Exhibit 7.1 illustrates one format for evaluating market opportunities by taking into consideration organizational resources. Each factor—production, marketing, finance, and management—is evaluated by rating it in relation to an opportunity on a scale of very good to very poor. The values assigned to each rating—5 for very good, 4 for good, and so on—permit quantifying the rating for each opportunity, which enables the analyst to compare several opportunities on a quantitative basis. Production, financial, and marketing personnel should be used to evaluate their respective functions in relation to

EXHIBIT 7.1. Company resource evaluation matrix.

Factors Evaluated	Very Good (5)	Good (4)	Fair (3)	Poor (2)	Very Poor (1)
			Rating		
Production					
Physical facilities					
Labor skills					
Technological capabilities					
Raw material supplies					
Production value					
Marketing					
Marketing skills					
Distribution facilities					
Channel availability					
Marketing score					
Finance					
Fixed capital requirements					
Work capital requirements					
Return on investment					
Finance score					
Management					
Number					
Depth					
Experience					
Total rating					

Source: Adapted from Stewart H. Rewoldt, James R. Scott, and Martin R. Warshaw, *Introduction to Marketing Management.* Homewood, IL: Richard D. Irwin, Inc., 1977, pp. 257, 261.

each opportunity. An alternate approach is to analyze these resources in relation to the opportunity as a strength or weakness. As is shown in Table 7.1 for each strength and weakness identified, strategic implications are drawn.

TABLE 7.1. Analysis of strengths and weaknesses.

	Factor	Opportunity Implication
Marketing Resources		
Strengths	Established channels of distribution for consumer products.	New product could use the same channels.
Weaknesses	No in-house advertising personnel and dependence on agency relationship.	Product needs strong advertising effort; must use ad agency.
Financial Resources		
Strengths	Good cash position and strong price/earnings ratio.	Consumers need installment plans.
Weaknesses	Higher than average debt to equity ratio.	Must fund through internal sources.
Physical Resources		
Strengths	High level of quality control technology.	Go for quality end of market.
Weaknesses	Long downtimes for product designs.	Must offer limited changes.
Managerial Resources		
Strengths	Strong process research and development staff.	Cost effectiveness in production.
Weaknesses	No experience with product.	Hire new management team.

Analysis of strengths and weaknesses flows logically from the identification of these resources relative to the opportunity. Each of these resources, when evaluated within this framework, can be labeled as a strength or weakness and the implications of that strength or weakness on a specific opportunity must be evaluated.

RANKING OPPORTUNITIES

Exhibit 7.2 presents a worksheet for summarizing the results of the analysis and for ranking the various market opportunities. Develop a comprehensive view of each opportunity by looking at all the various

EXHIBIT 7.2.
Summary of opportunity analysis worksheet.

	Opportunity Identification	
	Characteristics of Opportunity 1	Characteristics of Opportunity 2
Factors analyzed:	Basic questions answered:	Opportunity rank:
Environmental	Are the general factors in the environment favorable to this market opportunity?	
Market	What are the specific market factors and are they favorable to this opportunity?	
Market potential	How many consumers are in this opportunity and what are potential sales?	
Competitive analysis	Do we have or can we have differential advantage in this opportunity?	
Revenue/cost analysis	Do we have a good estimate of the revenues and costs involved?	
Profitability analysis	What level of capital expenditures are needed to compete successfully? What is the potential ROI?	
Alignment with purpose/mission	Would going after this opportunity be in line with the overall purpose/mission?	
Alignment with resources: Marketing Production Finance Managerial	Do we have or can we acquire the marketing, financial, production, and managerial resources required by this opportunity?	
Other factors: Economic Technological Political and legal Cultural and social	Are each of these factors favorable or unfavorable in relation to each opportunity?	
Total score		

elements which have been analyzed together rather than examining one element—market potential, for example—and then making a decision on the basis of that one factor. No one factor alone determines the attractiveness of an opportunity but the composite of all factors together.

To help quantify the attractiveness of the various opportunities, numbers can be assigned to each on each factor evaluated. For example, if four opportunities are evaluated, the numbers 1 through 4 can be used to rank each opportunity on a given factor. If two opportunities appear to be equal on a given factor, the same number is assigned to each opportunity to indicate tied valuations. If lower numbers are used to indicate higher rankings, that is, 1 represents the highest rank, the opportunity with the lowest overall score represents the most desirable opportunity for the firm.

As was pointed out earlier, it is not a matter of choosing only one opportunity. A firm with adequate resources may choose several and proceed to develop strategies appropriate for each. The result of this type of analysis is recognition of the differences between opportunities and what this implies in terms of strategies and resources required by a given opportunity.

DEVELOPING A WRITTEN BUSINESS PLAN

In any new endeavor requiring external funding, a formal business plan must be prepared. The plan need not be a dissertation, but it must contain enough information to allow a representative of a potential source of funds to evaluate the project realistically. The written business plan serves as a communication device with those sources of funds and must be clear, complete, and concise.

A comprehensive business plan contains a cover letter, a description of the business, a marketing plan, a technical plan of operations, a financial plan, and a management plan. Each portion outlines precisely what the business person proposes to do.

Cover Letter

The cover letter is the last part of the business plan to be written. The letter indicates the dollar amount of funding proposed, the terms and timing of the funding, and the type and value of collateral offered.

Business Description

The business description will contain a specific statement of the objectives of the business. The primary emphasis should be on profitability. Funding sources are not particularly interested in community service goals such as providing employment. Lenders know that a business will achieve the maximum reasonable employment if entrepreneurs attend to profitability goals. Such goals are usually stated as a rate of return on sales, a rate of return on investment or assets, or maximizing profits (long- or short-term).

The name of the business is included in this section of the plan. A good name which indicates who the business is and what it does should be used. The proposed location(s) of the business including pertinent size information is necessary. A plant, store, or service layout to scale helps explain a new business to the funding source.

At this stage, discuss in summary fashion the products or services the firm will provide to the market and the general nature of the target market including the area coverage of the business. This description should be sufficient to give a plan reviewer an understanding of what is proposed.

Marketing Strategy

This portion of the business plan should provide a description of the total market to be served and the industry trends. (This section allows a reviewer to decide whether or not you are entering a declining, stable, or growing industry.) There should be a clear statement of the market segments the business proposes to serve including relevant characteristics, the size of each market segment, the market potential of each segment, the sales potential for the firm or product in each segment, and the cost of sales and overhead expenses required to serve each segment. This information allows entrepreneurs to determine the approximate incremental (additional) profit which can be expected from each segment. The business should not attempt to market to unprofitable segments unless there are goals other than profitability. The firm can serve a market segment as long as the sales in that segment exceed the incremental costs of serving the segment and make some contribution to firm overhead.

Once the firm's market segment(s) have been clearly identified and located, an explanation of the marketing mix needed to serve each segment is necessary. The marketing mix for each segment will include the products or services offered that segment, the method of distribution or location for each segment, the price each segment will be expected to pay, and the promotion strategy that will be used to communicate with each market segment.

Technical Plan

This portion of the plan will be developed differently for retail, service, contracting, and manufacturing firms.

Retail plan. A retail plan outlines the physical facilities necessary to operate the store. This plan will include a drawing of the facility, a list of furniture, fixtures, and equipment needed in the store. An outline of the amount and type of inventory required and sources of supply will be necessary.

Service plan. The service plan will outline the physical facilities and equipment needed to operate the business. In addition, an outline of each service offered should be provided. A time schedule for the operation of the business should be provided. The inventory of a service business is time and talent.

Contracting plan. A contracting firm should outline exactly what types of contracts will be sought and how, the resources and processes needed to perform on the contracts including bonding requirements, and time frames that will be used in the contracting business.

Manufacturing plan. Manufacturing plans include the manufacturing operations, the raw materials needed and sources of supply, the equipment needed and sources or supply, labor skills needed, space required, and overhead items needed such as maintenance equipment.

Contact the local Small Business Administration office for Management Aids: 2.007 for manufacturers, 2.008 for construction, 2.022 for service firms, and 2.020 for retailers planning guides; or contact your local Small Business Development Center for assistance.

Financial Plan

The financial plan will probably be the first portion of the plan a reviewer will consider in detail. For that reason, this section of the business plan requires particular attention. The financial plan contains a pro forma balance sheet or pro forma statement of financial condition. The term pro forma means a projected form of some statement. Four pro forma balance sheets are in the plan: one before opening or starting the project, and one at the end of each of the first three years of operation. The pro forma balance sheet contains a list of fixed and current assets and their purchase prices. Precise verifiable estimates for all asset values are required. Estimates should be avoided. Estimating the value of a company car at $18,000 is not acceptable. The entrepreneur should go to a car dealer, negotiate a price for a specific car, and get a statement from the dealer regarding the negotiated price.

Fixed assets include building and land, equipment, furniture, fixtures, tools, and other assets which last more than a year and are depreciated. Current assets (working capital) include cash, inventory, and accounts receivables and other assets that will or can be converted to cash without harming the business in some period less than a year. These assets are called working capital because they work to earn the profits of the business. Cash becomes inventory, inventory becomes accounts receivable, and accounts receivable becomes cash. Cash to cash is the working capital cycle or turn.

The other portions of the pro forma balance sheet are the liabilities section and the equity section. Debt and equity are the two sources of funds to pay for the assets needed to conduct the business. The entrepreneur will be expected to have between 25 and 50 percent of the value of assets to inject into the business. This injection will have to be cash or property to be used in the business. Equity should not be confused with collateral. Collateral will be discussed later in this chapter. The entrepreneur's equity injection is considered a long-term investment in the business. These funds will be the last funds paid out of the business when it closes.

Debt is money or other resources you will borrow to pay for the remainder of the assets required for the business. Banks and suppliers are major sources of debt financing. Under normal circumstances, this portion of the firm's financing cannot exceed 80 percent of the value of assets.

The pro forma balance sheet shows the firm's assets and how they will be financed including how much the entrepreneur is proposing to borrow and how much equity the entrepreneur will need. After the balance sheet is completed, the entrepreneur will need to develop a pro forma income statement for the first year. Pro forma income statements were discussed in Chapters 5 and 6. The first step in preparing a pro forma income statement is developing a sales forecast. The project sales forecast should provide monthly estimates of sales for the first three years of the firm's existence. The first number questioned by funding sources is the sales forecast. The entrepreneur must be able to document and justify the sales forecast. Market demand analysis and sales forecasting are discussed in Chapter 3.

The pro forma income statement provides funding source reviewers with estimated sales; the cost of sales; operating expenses such as rent, advertising, wages and salaries, taxes, depreciation, interest expense and so on; and profit before taxes. Entrepreneurs can estimate each item on the income statement for the whole year and divide them up over twelve months to get monthly estimates for the first year.

Accountants use a concept called matching in preparing income statements. What that means is that income statements show sales and then match the expenses required to generate those sales against them. Some expenses will vary with sales (e.g., sales commissions); other expenses (e.g., depreciation) will be the same each month. The pro forma income statement should fairly accurately reflect the expenses incurred to generate each month's sales.

With personal computers and spreadsheet software, pro forma income statement preparation is greatly simplified. The pro forma monthly income statements become a budget that should be used to monitor the firm's financial performance. With a spreadsheet it is easy to prepare monthly income statements for each of the first three years.

After the pro forma income statements are complete, a cash flow statement can be prepared. Cash receipts from cash sales and collections from receivables can be estimated from information contained in the pro forma balance sheets and pro forma income statements. Cash disbursements include all expenses for which a check is written each month plus other items for which checks are written but which may not be included in the income statement. These other items for which cash is paid include the amount of each loan payment, which includes principal and interest. The interest portion of the payment is included in the income statement, but it is necessary to pay the interest plus principal in the note payment. Similarly, items such as insurance are typically paid in full at the beginning of the year and represent a cash disbursement in that month and in no other month but are written off in equal installments on the income statement. Cash receipts minus cash disbursements each month yields net cash flow. Net cash flow can be added to beginning cash to get cash available.

The pro forma cash flow statements indicate the firm's ability to meet its obligations as they come due. These statements are going to be extremely important to funding sources and should be prepared with care. Pro forma cash flow statements will need to be prepared by month for the first year and by year for the second and third years. With spreadsheet capability, monthly cash flow statements are easily prepared.

A pro forma cash flow statement was shown in Table 5.1. Notice that the income statement shows only interest expense and the cash flow statement shows the principal payment including both interest and principal. The insurance payment shown in the first month of the cash flow statement is shown divided up equally over twelve months in the income statement. All these projections should be explained in detail with assumptions clearly stated.

A funding-source reviewer would begin analysis of the pro formas with key financial ratios. The debt to equity ratio will be calculated to determine if the firm has an adequate equity injection. The quick ratio, acid test ratio, inventory turn ratio, and accounts receivable turn will be among the ratios used to determine whether the projections made seem reasonable. These ratios indicate the firm's ability to cover its obligations as they come due and how well assets are going to be used in the business. Other ratios used will include return on equity, return on assets, and return on sales. These latter ratios indicate the projected profitability of the venture. The ratios in the business plan will be compared by a reviewer to established industry ratios available from sources such as *Annual Statement Studies* (Robert Morris and Associates), *Industry Norms & Key Business Ratios* (Dun and Bradstreet) or *Almanac of Business and Industrial Financial Ratios* (Prentice Hall), and *Financial Studies of the Small Business* (Financial Research Associates). A well-developed plan will provide this ratio analysis for the reviewer.

The last portion of the financial plan will include a straightforward presentation of the collateral available to support the loan if that is to be the source of funding. Collateral is money or property available to repay the loan if the business fails. Collateral includes the business's assets as well as other assets owned by the principals which can be pledged. If the value of available collateral exceeds the amount necessary, the entrepreneur should avoid, if possible, specifically pledging more. In negotiating, the entrepreneur should attempt to pledge specifically listed collateral for the loan. Although the endorsement of all principals technically pledges everything, a list allows the entrepreneur some freedom in negotiating for other needed funds. The entrepreneur can purchase mortgage or life insurance and pledge the proceeds as collateral. Funding sources often require such life insurance.

If the proposed project is an expansion, the entrepreneur will follow the procedure outlined but include the new activity requirements in the pro forma balance sheets, income statements, and cash flow statements.

Management Plan

Funding source reviewers will take a long hard look at the people who are proposing to start a new venture or expand an existing venture. Management failures are the underlying cause of 92 percent of business failures according to Dun and Bradstreet. For that reason, detailed résumés for each principal in the venture will need to be prepared. The resume should include personal data, educational data, and work experience. Particular attention should be given to any managerial or leadership activities the entrepreneur has been involved in including those while the entrepreneur was in college. Being a leader while in a fraternity or university student government, for example, is an important indicator of managerial and leadership capacity. At some point, personal interviews of the principals may be requested by funding sources. Bankers have a saying, "If you have an entrepreneur with a great idea and mediocre management skills, or an entrepreneur with a mediocre idea and good management skills, go with management skills."

Form of Business Organization

The legal form of business organization is important to funding sources and should be discussed in the business plan. The firm could be a sole proprietorship. In many instances, this legal form of organization is adequate. If the firm is going to be a small store and will have only minor risk exposure for employees and customers, a "slip and fall" insurance policy can be used to cover the sole proprietorship.

Sometimes two or more people will form a partnership to begin a business. The partnership agreement should be in writing and attached to the business plan. Since all partners are jointly and severally liable for the firm's obligations, personal financial statements on all principals with more than 20 percent interest in the venture will be required by most funding sources. A sample personal financial statement available at local commercial banks should be included in the plan. The first page is a summary of information and the second page is a detailed outline of the information contained on the first page.

Incorporation is a common method of dealing with multiple owner ventures. Although some entrepreneurs think that they will be able to avoid personal liability for the firm's obligations associated with partnerships, common practice among lending institutions is to have all principals endorse all corporate notes. This requirement means that each principal, even in corporations, is still responsible for all the firm's obligations. If the firm is incorporated, the articles of incorporation and bylaws may be requested by funding sources.

Funding sources will want to know who is on the board of directors of the corporation and may require résumés on nonowner board members. This information allows the funding source to assess the management capacity of nonowner board members.

An organization chart of the business should be included in the business plan. This allows funding source reviewers to see who will be leading and managing the firm, who the middle managers are, and what type of employees will be needed in the firm. A fairly detailed staffing plan including job descriptions, number of employees, and employee qualifications needed should be a part of the business plan.

Finally, an operating plan for the next two years should be included. This plan will outline what you expect to do in operations during the first three months of the new venture (e.g., acquire financing, construct facility, install equipment, or hire and train employees). The operating plan would then shift to the beginning of operations phase. Here you would explain the beginning of operations (purchase materials or inventory, have a "shakedown" run, and working up to full speed) over the next six to nine months. As the venture gets up-to-speed, outline in general the continuing activities of the firm in a typical week or month. This portion of the plan will vary by type of business—retail, service, construction, and manufacturing have very different operating plans. In the operating plan, potential difficulties or problems should be outlined with a plan to deal with those difficulties and problems.

Entrepreneurs should visit two or three similar firms (not necessarily exactly like the one being proposed, but operationally similar) where the owners will not see them as competitors to get information "straight from the horses mouth." The three firms visited might include a fairly young business, one three or four years old, and a mature firm. A great deal of good operational information can be gleaned from such visits.

The various components of a business plan are very important and should be well-developed. Funding-source reviewers will pay primary attention to the financial plan. The marketing plan, the technical plan, and the management plan all provide evidence that the financial plan can be accomplished as proposed.

USES AND SOURCES OF FUNDS FOR NEW OR EXPANDING BUSINESSES

Uses of Funds

Although uses of funds were discussed in Chapter 5, a short review at this point will be helpful. In financial planning, four distinct time frames are important to the planning process. The entrepreneur should plan for start-up, survival, growth, and changing economic circumstances.

Start-up and cash. Start-up finance included the funds needed to buy the building and land (if desirable), equipment, furniture, fixtures, inventories, cash to meet regular immediate obligations, and for the investment in accounts receivables if credit is to be extended. Listing these and finding their respective values determines startup financing requirements.

Survival and cash. Most new ventures do not generate enough cash to cover their obligations immediately. For that reason, financially well-planned ventures include estimated survival cash. Survival cash is the amount needed to cover regular bills until the firm grows and begins generating enough cash to provide the coverage. Nothing on an electricity bill states, "If you don't sell enough this month, don't worry about this bill." The entrepreneur must arrange for enough cash when negotiating initial financing to cover survival cash. The cash flow pro forma statements discussed in Chapter 6 will reveal the period during which negative cash flows will require survival cash. Although survival cash is negotiated before the business is started, it will not be used and should not be borrowed until it is needed. For that reason, get a written agreement from the funding source covering your future survival cash needs. There are fewer worse situations than having an oral agreement with your banker to cover these needs and when you go in to get the funds there is a black wreath on the banker's door.

Growth and cash. As a firm grows, particularly if the growth is fast, cash needs grow. It may be necessary to fund new buildings, equipment, furniture, fixtures, inventory, and receivables. The well-managed business anticipates such requirements and arranges for whatever external funding the firm may require. Getting these funds may require a new business plan or an amendment to the old plan. In any case, growth cash may become necessary.

Changing economic circumstances and cash. As a new venture is launched, the entrepreneur must manage cash during the various phases of the business cycle. During the decline stage, the properly managed venture will cut back on inventory purchases and liquidate excess inventories, and because sales are declining, accounts receivables will be falling. These management activities will generate cash which should be conserved in marketable securities. During the recession phase of the business cycle, cash will be used and reserves are likely to fall. Even if expenses are cut, this situation will result if the recession persists because the firm has regular bills to pay and may be generating inadequate cash from sales and collections. During the recovery phase of the business cycle, additional cash will be required to cover inventory rebuilding and additional accounts receivables resulting from increased sales. Both the recession and recovery stages of the business cycle are cash users.

During the prosperity phase of the business cycle, cash reserves should improve. Some of the extra cash flow should be "salted away" into marketable assets to meet future requirements. It may be necessary to find external funds during the recovery stage of the business cycle since reserves may be depleted by the recession.

Sources of Cash

After the entrepreneur has estimated the specific uses of funds and determined what additional external funds are needed it will be necessary to *find* the necessary funds. Two external sources of funds available to the entrepreneur are equity and debt.

Equity Sources of Cash

Equity sources come from people or institutions that take partial ownership of the firm in return for funds to be used in financing the startup, survival, and/or growth of a new venture. These funds are long-term sources and should be used to finance the long-term needs of the firm. Long-term needs include fixed asset financing and permanent current assets financing for both start-up and growth. Since it is usually easier to borrow for fixed assets, these funds should be used to finance basic working capital and growth needs for both working capital and fixed asset financing.

Partnerships

One approach to increasing the funds available to finance a business is to extend ownership to others through partnerships. One of the major reasons for the invention of partnerships was to develop an additional source of funds.

Bringing in additional owners with cash resources is one way to get or improve the equity base of a firm. Of course, some control over the venture is lost by the entrepreneur to other partners. Profits or losses also will be shared with the new partners. Care should be taken in selecting partners to insure that they can contribute to the firm in a positive way. Consider selecting partners who can contribute to the management of the firm beyond their financial contributions.

Other forms of partnerships exist to help in special circumstances. Because of these special arrangements, the agreement should be in writing. In fact, all partnership agreements should be in writing. *Silent partners* contribute to the firm's finances and own a part of the business but do not want to participate in the management of the firm. Silent partners, however, can become quite vocal when their investment is jeopardized. *Secret partners* want to invest in the firm and participate in its profits, but do not want to be known to the public as partners. *Dormant partners* are both secret and silent.

Limited partners participate in the firm, but have their risk limited to their investment in the firm. They do not want the risks associated with a general partnership where partners are jointly (all together) and severally (each) responsible for the obligations of the firm.

Incorporation allows owners to participate in the firm but avoid the joint and several obligations of the partnership. Limited liability is one of the major advantages of incorporation. However, most funding sources for small businesses require personal endorsement by all principals of corporate notes. Thus, for small ventures at least (and most ventures are small), limited liability is not a realistic expectation.

The corporation allows the entrepreneur to sell shares of the company to others and raise capital. Whether or not this approach or the partnership approach can work depends entirely on the market for the partnership share or the shares of corporate stock. Shares of ownership (partner or corporate) for small new firms are not highly valued by the others and it is therefore difficult to raise capital unless others interested in buying part ownership can be identified (usually among close friends and family).

Limited liability company or partnerships are a new form of organization and are becoming more and more prevalent throughout the country. Basically these entities provide the limited liability of incorporation without the formality associated with the legal form.

Another problem with offering ownership that should be avoided is getting into trouble with the Securities and Exchange Commission. If shares of ownership are going to be offered to "unsophisticated" investors, it will be necessary to prepare a "Private Confidential Memorandum" for partnerships and a prospectus for incorporation, which can get quite expensive. General offers should not be made until it is clear that large sums of equity capital are needed.

Partnerships and incorporation are useful approaches to raising equity capital. Equity capital equal to at least 20 percent of the proposition is necessary before debt sources will consider lending to a venture.

Another set of sources of equity capital include various types of *angel capitalists* and *venture capitalists* or *venture capital firms*. Angel capitalists are willing to invest in a new venture in anticipation of profits or other goals. Venture capitalists are willing to invest in a venture in anticipation of a profit or other goal.

Angel capitalists are individuals or small groups of individuals who are willing to finance new ventures in the very early stage of development. Because of the risks involved in their investments, they usually invest in opportunities with which they are familiar. In addition to providing funds, these individuals usually want to be directly involved with entrepreneurs in the business; often providing management and technical assistance.

Because of the risk involved, most venture capitalists want to look at opportunities have a track record and which need funds for the growth phase of the venture. The venture capitalist or the venture capital firm wants to ride through the rapid growth very profitable stage of the venture life cycle and get out at the top of this phase by selling their now much more valuable stock to the original entrepreneurs or others. The venture capitalist or venture capital firm then seeks another similar rapid growth opportunity. Some venture capitalists are willing to provide seed capital for venture start-ups. Mezzanine financing (between initial slow growth and the rapid growth phase of the firm) is also hard to arrange with venture capitalists or venture capital firms.

A few public-minded people use a part of their accumulated wealth to help get new ventures started as a community service. They are not universally available, but an entrepreneur may be able to find them through a local Chamber of Commerce or through traditional lending sources who probably know of such individuals.

The number of *seed capital* funding organizations is on the rise in the United States. These organizations, including private, public, and public/private partnerships, can fill a gap between the need for start-up, early slow growth, and mezzanine financing and the rapid growth financing available from venture capitalists and venture capital firms.

These organizations are being started by banks, utility companies, economic-development agencies, chambers of commerce, and others interested in economic development. In some areas, banks and others are starting *certified development companies,* which can provide seed capital to new ventures in various forms. *Local development companies,* sponsored by the Small Business Administration (SBA) are also available throughout the country. Similar entities funded by the Economic Development Administration are available to assist in funding the start-up, early slow growth, and mezzanine financing of ventures. Other local, regional, or state entities are being established to fill the gap in equity financing between entrepreneurs startup resources and the larger sums of money available after the firm has a track record.

Small business investment companies (SBIC), privately owned and licensed by the SBA, are another source of equity capital for startups and growth funding. A similar entity established to provide equity and debt funding for businesses owned by minorities or other socially or economically disadvantaged groups is the *minority enterprise small business investment companies (MESBIC).*

Debt Finance

Most new or expanding ventures find it difficult or impossible to raise all funds from equity sources. Many debt sources are available to entrepreneurs. These sources loan money to new and expanding ventures in the expectation that the funds will be repaid with interest. The interest rate can be low, but the expectation of repayment is still present.

As in equity sources, the first groups usually approached for debt financing are *close family and friends.* These sources are very important to many entrepreneurs. Funds borrowed from family and friends must not be a burden to them, otherwise problems will inevitably arise.

Banks are a major source of funds for new and expanding ventures. Historically, banks were considered short-term sources of funds. Term loans of up to five years were also possible. With deregulation, banks have become more versatile in their lending practices. Bankers continue to consider their role as providing short-term financing (up to five years) and find it difficult to lend for longer periods except under special circumstances.

Typical bank loans for inventory and receivables would not exceed the seasonal requirements (usually less than a year) of the business. A seasonal line of credit is a typical approach to such short-term funding. With tightened regulations, "evergreen" loans (loans that were short-term, but which were rolled over with interest repayment) can now be provided.

Because of the dynamics of the capital market, nontraditional lender/equity firms have come into existence. These nontraditional lenders have investors and are therefore not restricted by the same rules as banks. As a result, they can make riskier loans. These firms use the SBA guarantee programs in the same way as banks.

The U.S. Small Business Administration has become an important player in the debt market for new and expanding ventures. The *7(a)* loan program provides guarantee, participation, and direct loans for working capital and fixed asset financing. A guaranteed loan means that a participating bank agrees to loan the entrepreneur money with the SBA guaranteeing up to 90 percent of the loan. That means that the bank has only a 10 percent exposure and the deal is more doable. A participation loan means that some of the money in the loan comes from the bank and some from the SBA. Finally, a direct loan means that the SBA loans the money directly to the entrepreneur. Since the beginning of the Reagan administration, direct loans have been less and less available.

A second loan program, the *504,* is designed to help finance larger fixed assets for new and expanding ventures. These loans are typically participating with the bank providing a portion and the bank providing a portion of the loan funds. In both these programs, the entrepreneur is expected to have an adequate equity injection–usually 10 to 20 percent of the deal. All loan programs require an equity injection.

The SBA also has a *Prequalification Loan* program to support women- and minority-owned businesses, rural businesses, veteran-owned businesses, and businesses engaged in export trade.

The recent widespread interest in microenterprise development has prompted the SBA to encourage banks and other lending institutions to participate in the new *Mini Loan* program. This program envisions loans down to $5,000. Current participating and guaranteed loans are for $50,000 or more because of the cost of administering such loans. Whether the mini loan program will work remains to be seen.

The United States Department of Agriculture (USDA) has a *Business and Industry (B&I)* loan program which operates in the same fashion as the SBA *7(a)* program for residents of rural areas. Generally these loans are expected to be $250,000 or more.

The *Economic Development Administration (EDA)* provides funding for local loan programs through grants to political subdivisions and municipalities. These programs have been very confusing for typical entrepreneurs who think that grants are available to them. The grant programs such as the *community development block grant (CDBG)* is to the political subdivision which can then turn the grant into a revolving loan fund to aid in economic development. Entrepreneurs should check out these sources with the local or state representative of the EDA.

Most states now have established loan programs similar to the SBA programs. Typical programs include guaranteed, participating, and direct loans to entrepreneurs for start-up and expansion. In Louisiana, for example, loan programs administered by the Louisiana Economic Development Corporation encourage small business development. These loans can be guaranteed, participation, or direct loans.

The Enterprise Zone/Community program has resulted in many loan programs that serve one or several counties. Many local political subdivisions have loan programs designed to encourage small business development. For example, Morehouse Parish, Louisiana, has such a program.

The typical procedure for tapping any of the government based programs is to prepare a business plan (loan package) for presentation to your banker. If the bank can make the loan, the entrepreneur needs go no further. If the bank cannot make the loan without a guarantee or participation by some agency (usually because of the length of time the funds are for or because of weak collateral) the bank can ask for participation or a guarantee from some established agency. If the bank or other lending institution is not will to make to loan at all, the entrepreneur may seek a direct loan from the appropriate agency.

Many local groups are establishing loan programs from donated private funds and public-sector funds to aid in economic development. Local, county, and state governments are becoming very aggressive in providing loan programs for local start-up and growth ventures.

One interesting set of initiatives (private, public, and public/private sector funded) involves several loan programs patterned after the Grameen Bank model in Bangladesh. These programs loan very small amounts to individuals who have a microenterprise opportunity which would provide employment (full or part-time) to the entrepreneur and others. The loans are often done in lending groups that determine in some measure which member of the group gets a loan when.

Grant Sources

Although there are many grant programs from private and public sources, the authors are aware of only two such grant programs designed to aid in establishing for-profit businesses. The Small Business Innovation Research (SBIR) program and its state counterparts and the Individual Development Account (IDA) program available in some areas. The SBIR program was established to allow small business entrepreneurs to participate in the Federal technology procurement programs. Each federal agency (fourteen agencies participate) specifically solicits technology from small business entrepreneurs to meet the needs of that agency. The solicitation outlines the technology sought and provides an application form for Phases I, II, or III financing. Phase I financing provides up to $50,000 for successful applicants to develop the requested technology. Phase II provides $500,000 to aid in moving the technology toward commercialization, and in Phase III private capital must be used to bring the technology to the commercialization stage. Many states provide matching funds for successful SBIR applicants.

The IDA programs generally allow employed individuals to save up to $1,000 and match that amount 4 to 1. This provides $5,000 equity for the microentrepreneur. The IDA account also can be used for education and home ownership.

Entrepreneurs seeking sources of funds for the start-up of expansion of their venture can seek funding from equity and debt sources. Many programs are available to entrepreneurs with well-developed business plans and the necessary management skills necessary to implement the plan. To tap into these sources, the entrepreneur should explore what is available in his or her area through various agencies such as the local Small Business Development Center, Chamber of Commerce, or local economic development agencies. The personnel in these agencies deal with loans all the time and are probably familiar with the sources available locally.

SUMMARY

This chapter concludes the market opportunity analysis. The analyst should have developed a complete database on the environmental factors, market factors, competition, revenue, cost, and ROI. Decisions must be made at this point on which opportunities, if any, will be sought.

The database which can be developed by performing these types of analyses is the basis for making decisions and also helps in strategy selection. As new opportunities are identified, the analysis process described previously should become standard procedure and a prerequisite to decision making with respect to these opportunities.

Finally, this chapter addressed the need for a business plan and identified sources and uses of funds. When outside funding of projects is required, these documents are vital in raising needed capital. Most lending agencies require these documents as a part of the loan application process.

CASES

CASE CONTRIBUTORS

Phylis M. Mansfield, Assistant Professor of Marketing, Penn State University, Erie, Pennsylvania.

Jacquelyn Warwick, Professor of Marketing, Andrews University, Berrien Springs, Michigan.

Bruce E. Winston, Dean of the School of Leadership Studies at Regent University, Virginia Beach, Virginia.

Case 1

Watercrest Park

Robert E. Stevens
David L. Loudon
Bruce E. Winston

Jim Owens was under considerable strain as he worked on a marketing plan for his new employer, Watercrest, Inc. He completed a consumer survey and a rough draft of the plan but was still unsure of the details of the rest of the document. Time was a factor in his concern since the deadline was one week away.

The designers of Watercrest originally envisioned the park as an outdoor water-related recreational facility. It was to include a wave pool, waterslides, swimming pools, jogging trails, and several water rides. In addition, the plan included dressing rooms, a snack bar, a souvenir shop, a large space for sunbathing, and space for special events such as outdoor concerts. The idea seemed sound after a consulting group conducted a feasibility study that confirmed the original ideas on the need and potential profitability of the concept. The next step was to create enough interest in potential investors to raise the $4 million needed to launch the project.

However, Sid James, originator of the Watercrest project, wanted to supply potential investors with a copy of the feasibility study as well as a complete marketing plan to help convince them of the project's viability. Mr. James hired Jim Owens, a recent marketing graduate, to prepare the plan and help manage the facility when it opened.

Jim's early work was relatively easy because the consulting team collected much of the environmental and competitive data for the feasibility study. The parts of the plan Jim completed are shown in the following analysis, including a summary of the study revealing consumers' reactions to the proposed project.

Situation Analysis

Environmental Trends

Although the Watercrest concept is new and therefore does not have a history, recreation in general and water-related recreation specifically, has a long and interesting history. The following trends and forecasts for recreation were taken from recent industry literature:

- Americans have a growing preoccupation with outdoor recreation.
- Based on past trends, a doubling of recreational expenditures can be expected in the next eight to ten years.
- Expenditures for leisure activities are increasing faster than consumer spending as a whole.
- More and more people are moving to the Sun Belt; the South and Southwest are expected to be major growth areas, and people tend to be more recreationally active there.
- Leisure spending does not appear to be as heavily influenced by adverse economic conditions as other expenditures.
- Total leisure spending is expected to reach $250 billion by next year and $350 billion in five years.
- Admissions revenues for sporting events grew from $3.6 billion to $15 billion over the past five years.
- The most popular sport in the United States is swimming—some 103 million people regularly swim.
- Water-related activities account for five of the top twenty-five outdoor recreational activities.
- Experts say that participation in summer outdoor recreational activities is four times greater than forty years ago.
- Many theme parks are currently in trouble financially because of saturation, competition, and inflation.
- Experienced theme park operators have learned how to keep guests for several hours and offer many alternative ways to spend money.
- A major cost problem for theme parks is the attempt to add a newer, more thrilling ride every two years—at continuing inflated costs.
- Big Surf outdoor water recreation project is successful. It appeals mainly to youths, ages eight to twenty-three; very few families participate.

Although large theme parks have recently had financial trouble, an overall favorable climate exists for outdoor recreation ventures, and water-related activities in the Sun Belt historically have enjoyed a high probability of success.

Consumer Analysis

Table C1.1 lists potential market segments for Watercrest. Two major characteristics of the market segments influenced planned marketing activities.

One was the size of the parties involved. Research from this project confirms that the primary markets for this project are youths and single adults. Also, many consumers indicate they would probably go with a group to this type of attraction. Although the plan will not ignore families, the size of the family segment, compared to the other two, warrants less marketing effort.

Another market-segment variable that the plan must consider is "resident versus tourist." Again, the plan will not ignore the tourist segment but primary emphasis will focus on the resident segment because of the size and accessibility of this group. Research reveals that the major motives for going to this type of park are:

1. *Fun:* a key word used by many consumers.
2. *Peers:* people like to be with others of their own age.
3. *Physical attraction of combination of sun and water:* people like to be near water in hot weather.
4. *Boredom:* people want other activities than staying home, watching television, and so on.

Consumers appear willing to spend five to eight dollars per person for this type of activity, and most youths report spending fifteen to twenty dollars a month on outdoor recreational activities during the summer.

There also appears to be a high degree of consumer acceptance of water-related activities such as waterslides. Most youths have been to a waterslide and most adults with children are aware and approve of waterslides. This translates to a favorable consumer mind-set for Watercrest.

The demographics of the market are favorable in terms of the major segments of Watercrest customers. Table C1.2 shows the size of the market by age. Population projections show a near doubling of the area population in the next twenty years.

Income statistics for the proposed location also reveal a very strong market. Table C1.3 shows a recent estimate of household buying income and the comparative local-state-nation percentage. Income in the area is not much different from the state. Overall, the area provides a stable economic base with future population growth and income levels that support additional recreational facilities.

TABLE C1.1. Market segments.

Type of Party	Size of Party		
	Individuals/Couples	Families	Groups
Area residents	Youths ages 8-18, single adults ages 19 and over, young couples	Young/no children, older/young children, older/older children	Church, college groups
Tourists	Single adults, young couples	Young/no children, older/young children, older/older children	Church, school groups

TABLE C1.2. Population distribution by age group.

Age Group	Total Number
6-17	70,758
18-34	150,134
35-64	92,700

TABLE C1.3. Household income (last census).

Income ($)	Proposed Location (%)	State (%)	United States (%)
Up to 15,000	26.4	27.3	25.4
15,001-25,000	7.3	6.9	6.6
25,001-35,000	17.5	17.6	18.0
35,001-45,000	26.9	28.7	30.8
45,001 and over	21.9	19.5	19.2

Competitive Analysis

Although there are many competing recreational activities in the area, none offers a facility comparable to Watercrest. In fact, at current prices for waterslides in the area, Watercrest should draw most consumers because of the cumulative attraction of other Watercrest activities and the positive Watercrest value. Each alternate recreational facility is a competitor for Watercrest; but given the nature of the project, there is no major daytime or nighttime competitor to Watercrest. Competitive data are shown in Tables C1.4 and C1.5.

Although Jim had laid the groundwork for the rest of the marketing plan, he was still unsure about which overall positioning strategy to use and how to effectively promote the park to generate enough sales to make the venture profitable. If the profitability of this venture followed other theme parks, high volumes of sales could be expected during the first two to three years. This would be followed by declines as competition increased and the novelty of the park made it less attractive to customers. His attendance projections are shown in Table C1.6.

TABLE C1.4. Indoor recreational daytime competitors.

Types	Number	Average Price
Theaters	23	$4.50/12 years and over
Skating rinks	4	$1.50/person
Bowling alleys	5	$1.70/person
Racquetball courts (public)	2	$5.50/person
Arcades	10	$0.25/game
Pistol ranges	3	$2.00/person

TABLE C1.5. Outdoor recreational daytime competitors.

Types	Number	Average Price
Waterslides	2	$2.00/30 minutes
		$3.50/1 hour
		$6.00/all day
Race cars	1	$1.25/lap
		Usually $10/person
Skateboard parks	1	$2.50/3 hours
Swimming pools (public)	6	$1.60/person
Miniature golf	3	$2.00/person
Tennis courts (public)	6	$2.00/person
Amusement parks	2	3-4 tickets per ride ($1.00)

Sid James indicated that the investors would be expecting at least a 15 percent return on investment for the $2 million dollar costs associated with fixed and operating capital needed for the park. Since there would be high fixed costs, the key to profitability was generating a high level of sales for the park.

TABLE C1.6. Attendance projections.

Facts/assumptions	Attendance Alternative first-year forecasts		
	Low	Most likely	High
Attendance/penetration Local market—target population Target market (ages 10-25)	112,000	112,000	112,000
Penetration	.65	.70	.85
Attendance	72,800	78,400	95,200
Local market—general population			
Population	103,087	103,087	103,087
Penetration	.03	.05	.07
Attendance	3,100	5,100	7,200
Regional market			
Population	90,000	90,000	90,000
Penetration	.10	.15	.20
Attendance	9,000	13,500	18,000
Tourist market			
Population	225,000	225,000	225,000
Penetration	.03	.05	.07
Attendance	6,750	11,250	15,750
Group sales market			
Attendance	18,275	20,350	25,700
Repeat business			
attendance	72,800	78,400	95,200
Total attendance (sum of above)	182,725	207,000	257,050

Low forecast: $1,827,250 (182,725 × $10); most likely: $2,070,000 (207,000 × $10); high forecast: $2,570,500 (257,050 × $10).

CASE APPENDIX

The Consumer Study

This section of the report discusses the methods for collecting consumer information and presents the results of the consumer study. Assessment of consumer attitudes on this new concept began with a series of focus-group interviews. Each focus group included twelve teenagers between the ages of twelve and eighteen. The males and females were evenly mixed, and most of the participants would be considered opinion leaders to some extent.

The interviews proceeded from a general discussion of recreation to outdoor activities to water-related activities. The moderator asked participants to comment on the Watercrest concept as well as many questions about participation, price, repeat trips, and so on. The consumer survey confirmed the findings of the focus group interviews and revealed a consistent pattern of responses from both data collection techniques. The method and findings of the consumer survey follow.

Introduction

Purpose. The purpose of this study was to provide data for market analysis and planning for the Watercrest project. The study provided data and a wide range of topics related to outdoor recreational activities and market participation.

Research objectives. This study sought to accomplish several research objectives:

- Identify the type of recreational activities residents participate in and the extent of participation by family unit.
- Determine the price levels anticipated by consumers for an outdoor recreational activity such as Watercrest.
- Determine exactly which consumer segment was most likely to be attracted to the project.
- Identify reasons for anticipated participation or lack of participation in the proposed project.
- Identify socioeconomic characteristics of the anticipated target markets.

Methodology

Sampling. Researchers selected respondents for this study through a cluster-sampling procedure of area residents listed in the current telephone book. The original clusters consisted of 1,500 residential listings. This rather large number was necessary to produce a sample of 300 respondents—225 adults and 75 young people. The researchers anticipated problems such as (1) disconnected numbers, (2) respondents who would not cooperate, and (3) potential respondents who could not be reached. Therefore the sample needed to begin with a large number of residents to ensure the desired sample size.

Survey Instrument and Data Collection

The researchers developed a telephone questionnaire and pre-tested it for validity. The following topics were covered in the survey:

- Participation in outdoor recreational activities
- Types of outdoor activities participated in
- Vacationing recreational activities
- Total family expenditures anticipated for an outdoor activity
- Familiarity with and reaction to waterslides
- Motivation for participation in water-related recreational activities

Socioeconomic Classification Data

The study used a separate questionnaire for young people to ensure collection of data from consumers most likely to use a recreational facility such as Watercrest. Researchers collected data during the second week of February using interviewers selected and trained by the consultants. Although the interviewers encountered little difficulty in obtaining cooperation or administering the questionnaires, many interviews were aborted completely because respondents were not participants in outdoor activities or were unfamiliar with water-related activities. The average adult interview took ten minutes for completion while the youths' interviews took approximately five minutes.

Data Tabulation and Analysis

The data were tabulated by computer and organized by topical area. The researchers calculated descriptive statistics to represent the basic response modes of consumers and permit further analysis of the data.

Findings

Outdoor recreational participation. Most of the respondents interviewed in the study (71 percent) participated in outdoor recreational activities with the most popular being swimming, jogging, and tennis. These data are consistent with earlier findings from the focus group interviews. Outdoor activity was clearly seen as an activity for youths by both adults and young people interviewed.

The majority of adults with children indicated a preference for staying and watching their children participate in an activity if the facility offered a comfortable place. Adults also seemed extremely concerned with safety for their children in this type of activity. Eighty-five percent of the respondents identified safety as their major concern.

Expenditure Data

Respondents were asked how much they would spend per person to participate in an outdoor recreational activity if they could stay for eight to ten hours as a family. The median response was $8.00 per person. When asked how much they would be willing to spend for one of their children to participate, the average response was $10.50. Youths' average response was $10.00 when asked the same question.

The current price for an all-day pass at a waterslide in the area is $6.00. Youths reported spending an average of $26.00 per month for recreational activities during the summer.

Socioeconomic Characteristics of Respondents

A typical adult respondent in this study can be profiled as follows:

1. Median income of a little over $25,000
2. About thirty years old
3. Male
4. Caucasian
5. Works in a professional or technical occupation
6. Median level of education was some college work completed

The majority of youths interviewed were between the ages of twelve and seventeen.

Summary and Conclusions

Based on the findings outlined in this study, the following conclusions and summary statements emerged:

• The majority of adults and youths view water-related activities such as a waterslide as being for young people—not for families or older adults.

- A price of ten to twelve dollars or more for the Watercrest complex is entirely in line with what adults and youths would expect to pay.
- The major reason for participation in water activity is summed up in one word—fun. Also, hot weather and water activities appear to be part of the consumer mind-set.
- The major concern of adults for this type of activity is safety in use.
- Most youths appear to be interested in participating in this type of activity with a group of friends.

Findings of this study parallel the earlier focus group interviews—a consistent pattern of responses in viewing outdoor recreational activities.

Many families are involved in outdoor recreational activities when at home and while on vacation. However, the variety of activities is much more limited when on vacation.

Case 2

Superior Electrical Contractors: Residential Services Division

Robert E. Stevens
David L. Loudon
Bruce E. Winston

As Jim Bell, owner of Superior Electrical Contractors, studied monthly sales figures for the last three months, what he feared he would see became clear. Last year, sales declined 37 percent and the year before those sales declined 20 percent. In light of this trend, Jim questioned the survival of his firm. He believed that the firm could survive if the newly created Residential Services Division could bring in the sales lost in the commercial market.

Background

Jim Bell began Superior Electrical Contractors eleven years ago in a medium-sized city in the South. The company's primary service was electrical wiring of commercial buildings. As a secondary line, the firm also sold and serviced residential and commercial heating and air-conditioning units. Since the company's inception, electrical contracting services had accounted for 70 percent of sales with the remaining 30 percent coming from the sales and service of heating and air-conditioning units. Routine maintenance services in the secondary line included Freon checks, filter replacements, and system repairs.

Most commercial electrical contracting work is given to the firm with the lowest bid on the project. Superior Electrical prepared each bid from electrical specifications furnished by the general contractor, or in a few cases, the client/company itself. If Superior submitted the winning bid, it would receive the contract and had to complete all work within the specified time at the bid price. Jim developed his own computer applications to assist in preparing cost estimates that helped him achieve a 98 percent average accuracy on job cost estimates.

Sales History

Superior Electrical Contractors grew from a sales volume of less than $100,000 in the first year to over $900,000 within a period of four years. Years six through nine showed sales figures holding consistent at around $1 million; however, as the state's economy faltered, sales volume declined. Figure C2.1 shows sales figures for the company. Although Superior's market share remained the same, there simply were not enough new jobs to bid. Tables C2.1 and C2.2 show the company's income statements for the past two years and the current balance statement.

Jim realized that he had to do something to reverse the trend in sales volume. The company began this fiscal year with the lowest level of contract work since the firm's first year of operation. He was convinced that the firm had to either expand the geographic area that the company operated in to find additional commercial work or find new sources of revenue in the current geographic area.

The Residential Services Division

Although the company generated some revenue each year from sales and services performed for residential customers, this business

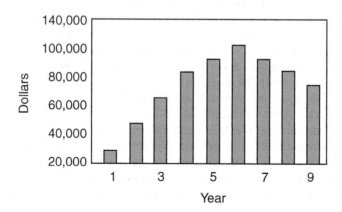

FIGURE C2.1. Superior's sales by year.

TABLE C2.1. Comparative statements of income and expenses for the most recent year ended June 30.

	Two Years Ago		Last Year	
	Percentage	Dollars	Percentage	Dollars
Income				
Contract income	100.00	937,317	100.00	594,624
Direct job costs				
Materials	41.15	385,716	39.42	234,417
Labor	23.24	217,870	25.13	149,404
Payroll taxes	2.64	24,739	2.66	15,795
Truck and travel	2.04	19,117	2.32	13,772
Subcontract	.42	3,950	1.64	9,744
Equipment rental	2.26	21,141	2.06	12,259
Miscellaneous	1.23	11,487	.08	556
Total direct job costs	72.98	684,020	73.31	435,947
Gross profit	27.02	253,297	26.69	158,677
Operating expense	26.88	251,958	37.94	225,591
Income (loss) from operations	.14	1,339	(11.25)	(66,914)
Other income				
Interest income	.18	1,700	.03	168
Gain on sale of fixed assets	.21	1,930	.00	—
Total other income	.39	3,630	.03	168
Income (loss) before taxes	.53	4,969	(11.22)	(66,746)
Federal and state income taxes	.00	.00	.00	.00
Net income (loss)	.53	4,969	(11.22)	(66,746)

was never aggressively developed or promoted. The firm always viewed this work as a way to keep crews busy between contracted jobs. Many competitors in this market perform a variety of electrical services for home owners, such as (1) light/fan fixture installations, (2) repair/replacement of electrical switches and breakers, as well as (3) sales and service of heating and air-conditioning units.

TABLE C2.2. Balance sheet, June 30, last year.

	Value
Current assets	
Cash in bank	$10,030
Accounts receivable—employees	216
Accounts receivable—trade	54,571
Materials inventory	54,667
Costs and estimated earnings in excess of billings	14,575
Prepaid expenses	8,890
Total current assets	$142,949
Fixed assets, at cost	
Machinery and equipment	63,083
Accumulated depreciation	(55,936)
Net fixed assets	7,147
Other assets	
Note receivable—officer	11,072
Stock, at cost	500
Refundable deposits	300
Total other assets	11,872
Total assets	161,968
Current liabilities	
Accounts payable	$23,942
Payroll taxes payable	3,068
Accrued interest	2,459
Accrued insurance	5,517
Notes payable—bank	103,160
Billings in excess of cost and estimated earnings	79
Total current liabilities	$138,225
Long-term liabilities	
Notes payable—bank	82,393
Total liabilities	220,618

	Value
Stockholders' equity	
Common stock	33,520
Treasury stock	(3,380)
Retained earnings	(88,790)
Total stockholders' equity	(58,650)
Total liabilities and stockholders' equity	161,968
Balance at beginning of year—July 1, two years ago	(22,044)
Add: Net income (loss)	(66,746)
Balance at end of year—June 30, last year	(88,790)

A customer experiencing an electrical problem would usually use the yellow pages to locate an electrical sales/service firm or rely on word-of-mouth recommendations from friends and neighbors. If customers were satisfied with the electrical sales/service firm, they would continue to call the same firm as other needs arose.

The idea for increasing the emphasis on the residential market came about by necessity but also through a conversation with another contractor at a national convention. This contractor explained to Jim that his firm had doubled its sales volume within two years by offering a maintenance contract to home owners. The maintenance contract provided: (1) two maintenance calls on each home to check out the central heating and air-conditioning system; (2) add refrigerant, if needed; (3) oil motors; (4) clean or replace filters; and (5) check for leaks and potential problems. The contract specified one filter and two pounds of refrigerant free per year. Customers paid for any additional supplies or parts required to repair a unit, separately upon approval to perform the work. The contractor said that he sold the maintenance contract for $99, which covered the cost of providing the service. However, additional services identified through the maintenance service, in addition to repeat business on other requested electrical services and word-of-mouth advertising, doubled his sales volume. The contractor told Jim that each maintenance contract generated an additional $300 in business and $150 in profits.

Jim asked a team of marketing students at the local university to conduct a survey to determine consumer interest in the idea of a maintenance contract. The results were very encouraging.

Market Survey Results

The survey of 100 area residents screened out non–home owners and home owners with homes valued at less than $75,000 to make sure the information represented higher-income consumers. Jim felt that the higher-income segment was most likely to respond favorably to such an offer. Those respondents who were extremely interested or somewhat interested were higher-income males with at least a college education (see Table C2.3).

Market Area Data

The market area served by Superior Electrical Contractors includes a population of 500,000 people and approximately 112,428 homes. Information from the tax assessor's office on the value of homes is shown in Table C2.4. Jim estimated that twenty percent of these homes were rental properties; however, he was certain that the rental homes were valued under $75,000. Jim believed that this left a large market potential for the maintenance agreement even with the under-$75,000 homes factored out.

Pricing Strategy Options

Jim believed that two alternative pricing strategies were available (see Table C2.5 for consumer price expectations). The first was a low price of under $100. This low price, though, would generate very little, if any, contribution to profit. However, a higher penetration of

TABLE C2.3. Level of consumer interest in maintenance agreement.

Response	Percentage
Extremely interested	11.1
Somewhat interested	50.0
Not at all interested	26.4
Don't know/not sure	12.5

TABLE C2.4. Tax assessment of home values (current year).

Home value	Number	Percent
Less than $25,000	3,375	3
$25,000 to $50,000	13,491	12
$50,001 to $75,000	25,857	23
$75,001 to $100,000	30,356	27
$100,001 to $125,000	20,236	18
$125,001 to $150,000	11,243	10
$150,001 to $175,000	4,497	4
$175,001 to $200,000	2,249	2
Over $200,000	1,124	1
	112,428	100

TABLE C2.5. Expected price for a maintenance agreement.

Expected annual price	Percentage
$50 or less	21.5
$51 to $75	26.9
$76 to $100	29.3
$101 to $125	16.2
$126 to $150	4.6
Over $150	1.5

homes would achieve greater exposure for Superior that might lead to additional revenue from other services.

The other strategy would price the agreement between $120 and $125 per customer generating between $20 and $25 contribution/ margin per customer. The trade-off would be lower market penetration and less opportunity to generate additional revenues from maintenance agreement customers.

Time was running out on choosing the right strategy. Jim had to call the printer so the price could be included in the brochure that was to be mailed to past customers. Jim was undecided on how best to promote the service to other home owners. The brochure cost $1,500 for 1,000 copies and represented one-tenth of his advertising budget. In addition to selecting the media and the message, Jim also had to decide on how long to run the promotional campaign.

Gateway Medical Waste Transport of Colorado

Robert E. Stevens
David L. Loudon
Bruce E. Winston

Kathy West, vice president of marketing at Gateway Medical Waste Transport of Colorado, sat at her desk reading the home office's request for a strategic marketing plan for the next three years including pro forma income statements. She had thought about this project off and on for the past couple of months and now faced the daunting task of actually creating the overall strategy and the mix of personal selling and advertising. The home office expected substantial growth from the Colorado operation and Ms. West searched for growth options to meet the desired sales/profit levels.

Background

Medical waste first came to the attention of the general public in the 1980s when it washed up on New Jersey beaches. Because of the media exposure of this event and others pertaining to undesirable disposal practices as well as fear of AIDS, public hysteria resulted and pressure was put upon regulatory officials to develop comprehensive regulations to prohibit such occurrences. The Medical Waste Tracking Act (MWTA) of 1988 was passed requiring the federal Environmental Protection Agency (EPA) to begin an investigation to determine whether federal legislation was necessary. The EPA provided their findings in 1991 which led to federal regulations on medical waste disposal.

Also, the Occupational Safety and Health Administration (OSHA) has begun to fine waste generators for improper disposal practices within their facilities and most states have adopted some type of regulation pertaining to infectious waste disposal requirements. The concern was not just for human medical waste but also animal medical waste since farmers and ranchers inoculate animals including beef, pork, and poultry.

The MWTA initially applied to facilities in Connecticut, New Jersey, and New York. Illinois, Indiana, Michigan, Minnesota, Ohio, Pennsylvania, and Wisconsin also were included within the original scope of the MWTA but were permitted to, and each elected to, opt out of coverage. The federal government permitted other states to opt into coverage under the MWTA, but only Rhode Island and Puerto Rico elected to be included. The MWTA only covered medical waste generated in any of the covered states. Conversely, the MWTA did not cover medical waste transported from a noncovered state to a covered state for treatment and/or disposal.

The EPA issued regulations (MWTA regulations) listing applicable generators, identifying the wastes that had to be tracked, and outlining standards for separating, packaging, and labeling medical waste. Facilities producing less than fifty pounds of waste per month are exempt from the tracking requirements. The MWTA regulations impose record-keeping requirements on all generators, transporters, and destination facilities and each facility must maintain all tracking records for three years. The program requires the use of a specified uniform tracking form. Additional requirements and operating procedures are applicable to transporters, and treatment, storage and disposal facilities. Generators exporting medical waste to a foreign country for treatment, destruction, or disposal must receive written confirmation of receipt within forty-five days; otherwise, an exception report must be filed by the forty-sixth day.

Company History

Gateway Medical Waste Transport, Inc. (GMWT), emerged in late 1988 in response to concerns expressed by federal, state, and local regulators regarding biomedical waste disposal practices and their impact upon human health and the environment. At that time, in most market areas, only BFI Medical Waste Systems and/or Waste Management, Inc., offered biomedical waste management services; and, as a result, those companies enjoyed a near monopoly in the marketplace, which reflected itself in the prices charged by those companies.

Since signing its very first account in March 1989, GMWT has grown to be the largest provider of biomedical waste management services in the state of Oklahoma where it currently manages 450,000 pounds of biomedical waste per month.

GMWT opened a subsidiary office in Denton, Texas, in early 1990 and enjoyed significant success throughout the Dallas-Fort Worth market area. This branch presently contracts with 23 hospitals that generate a total of 150,000 pounds of biomedical waste each month. The Dallas-Fort Worth Hospital Council recently endorsed GMWT as the preferred provider of biomedical waste management services to its member hospitals. This endorsement should lead to greater presence in the market.

In addition to serving Oklahoma and Northern Texas, GMWT also presently services numerous medical facilities in Kansas, Missouri, Arkansas, Colorado, and Wyoming. GMWT received endorsement from Voluntary Hospitals of America (VHA) for its biomedical waste disposal service to VHA member facilities.

A major factor in the success of GMWT, in addition to its quality of service and competitive pricing, is the exclusive use of a newly constructed, fully permitted incinerator with a capacity of 100 tons per day. This incinerator was designed specifically for biomedical waste (including antineoplastic/chemotherapy wastes) and is located in Oklahoma. GMWT routinely arranges for potential clients to tour this impressive facility which instills confidence regarding the disposition of biomedical wastes.

The Colorado Department of Health recognized GMWT's stature as a major provider of biomedical waste management services when a Denver biomedical waste management company requested GMWT to assist in the immediate removal and incineration of nearly one million pounds of biomedical waste that the company had stored in trailers in the Denver area. GMWT successfully completed this project within the twenty-one-day compliance time frame imposed by Colorado authorities.

All GMWT employees directly involved in the hands-on management of biomedical wastes receive training in the proper use of personal protective equipment and appropriate corrective actions relating to spills, including decontamination techniques and procedures. All GMWT employees, including drivers, submit to GMWT's proactive substance abuse program, which includes drug testing upon employment and random testing thereafter. All GMWT drivers must also meet U. S. Department of Transportation driver qualification standards, including physical exams and an annual review of their driving records. In addition, GMWT employs a team of emergency responders who must complete a forty-hour emergency response course conducted by Oklahoma State University.

GMWT's corporate management includes an environmental attorney licensed by the state of California whose other credentials include a master's-level certification in hazardous materials management from the Institute of Hazardous Materials Management. He also serves as an adjunct extension program faculty member in environmental management at Oklahoma State University.

GMWT is permitted to manage biomedical materials including infectious wastes (wastes capable of producing an infectious disease), chemical wastes (such as pharmaceutical wastes), laboratory wastes, antineoplastic drugs, other chemicals, and those items that are not regulated as hazardous wastes. The infectious wastes that GMWT manages include the following:

1. Cultures and stocks of infectious agents and associated biologicals
2. Human blood and blood products
3. Pathological wastes
4. Contaminated sharps
5. Contaminated animal carcasses, body parts, and bedding
6. Wastes from surgery, autopsies, and other medical procedures
7. Laboratory wastes
8. Dialysis unit wastes
9. Isolation wastes unless determined to be noninfectious by the infection control committee at the health care facility
10. Any other material and contaminated equipment that, in the determination of the facility's infection control staff, presents a significant danger of infection because it is contaminated with, or may reasonably be expected to be contaminated with, etiologic agents. An *etiologic agent* is a type of microorganism, helminth, or virus that causes, or significantly contributes to the cause of, increased morbidity or mortality of humans.

The chemical wastes handled by GMWT include the following:

1. Pharmaceutical wastes
2. Laboratory reagents contaminated with infectious body fluids
3. All the disposable materials in contact with cytotoxic/antineo-plastic agents during the preparation, handling, and administration of such agents (Such waste includes, but is not limited to, masks, gloves, gowns, empty IV tubing bags and vials, and other contaminated materials.)
4. Other chemicals that may be contaminated by infectious agents as designated by experts at the point of generation of the waste

The Colorado Operation

GMWT opened a subsidiary office in Denver to provide quality, competitively priced biomedical waste management services to the medical community in Colorado. Mr. Rick Stewart and Ms. Kathy West manage this office. Ms. West was formerly employed by BFI in Oklahoma, where she helped set up its medical waste program and ranked first in sales and service throughout that company in its biomedical waste operations. Her background and training enabled her to assist medical facilities in their efforts to properly manage biomedical wastes in a safe and economical manner consistent with all regulations and joint commission guidelines. This office, in one three-month period, signed obligations generating enough revenue to cover 60 percent of the subsidiary's operating costs.

GMWT currently serves thirty-five clients in the eastern part of the state and will soon provide service to all of Colorado. The GMWT office located in Denver, Colorado, currently has a staff of four with vast experience in the areas of medical waste and transportation. GMWT of Colorado offers its clients a comprehensive medical waste management program and assists them in a consultative role. This includes assessment of their current system and recommendations for improvement. If a program does not exist, GMWT helps to develop one. This process can take several days for a large hospital or a few minutes for a small office. Once service begins, GMWT adds the clients onto a pick-up route that allows GMWT to conform to a schedule and gives the client assurance of timely service. GMWT provides all clients with containers for waste disposal and also documentation confirming receipt of waste and an actual date of incineration. GMWT currently uses a twenty-foot bobtruck, which collects the waste at the generator's site. At the end of a route, a trained technician transports the waste to GMWT's transfer facility and off-loads it into a fifty-three-foot trailer. When full, GMWT transports the trailer to the incinerator in Oklahoma. No operational incinerator currently exists in Colorado. Incineration is the only method of disposal that GMWT of Colorado uses.

For GMWT to be competitive, long-haul-transportation costs must stay at a minimum. GMWT currently uses Ranger Transportation, Inc., a nationwide transportation company that provides all trailers and transport to Stroud, Oklahoma, within a forty-eight-hour period from pickup. Ranger's drivers must complete a special spill-response training course.

Colorado presently requires generators to have a comprehensive infectious waste management plan in place, documentation of proper disposal, written standard operating procedures, and regular monitoring of the disposal practice. Noncompliance with these requirements subjects the generator to civil penalties.

Currently, ninety-one hospitals in Colorado generate a total of approximately 35,146 pounds of infectious waste per day. In addition, there are also several thousand physicians and dentists as well as hundreds of clinics, laboratories, and other infectious waste generators. About 73 percent of hospitals and 20 percent of clinics and others use commercial disposal companies (the clinics and others are just now beginning to use this type of service). This yields an average annual revenue potential of about $500,000.

Competition in the marketplace favors GMWT because of its strength in disposal capacity and capabilities, technology, service, track record, as well as expertise. BFI Medical Waste Systems (BFI), Waste Management, Inc. (WMI), and others operating in the area all acknowledge major weaknesses. BFI had been a tough competitor until recently when it made the decision to autoclave waste for Colorado rather than incinerate. *Autoclaving* involves steam sterilization of waste and disposal in a landfill. WMI also autoclaves as do the other competitors. GMWT, on the other hand, uses state-of-the-art incineration in Oklahoma and has a staff of specialized industry experts.

Marketing Activities

Marketing activities in Colorado have mirrored the activities used in other locations. GMWT has focused on personal selling since an on-site inspection of a generator's facility is required to determine whether it meets current codes for handling waste and the volume of waste on a monthly basis.

Colorado's sales force consists of three people who received specialized training in medical waste disposal issues. The salespeople provide comprehensive waste stream assessments, comparative cost analyses, intensive staff training in servicing, as well as ongoing consultation in regulatory compliance issues. GMWT had not yet contacted all the hospitals statewide. Ms. West thought that cold calling, as well as telemarketing support and a mail-out campaign might be the best way to reach the potential customers.

Financial Performance

GMWT of Colorado, Inc., is becoming more financially independent. Current accounts are generating enough revenues to cover approximately 60 percent of operating costs. With the addition of new accounts weekly, it projects a break-even point to occur within a six-month period based on calculations comprised of income statements and budget projections. Due to the nature of the business and the size of the market, GMWT of Colorado had forecasted a profit after the first year of business. Kathy West also feels that a 25 percent growth over the next three years is a very realistic projection for the company (see Table C3.1).

After the initial three years of growth, West expects increased competition and slower growth. She is concerned about the company's ability to continue this growth pattern and wonders how this might affect GMWT's ability to attract additional investors to support expansion. She also wonders about ensuring other strategic options that might be available rather than expanding the business to other geographical areas.

TABLE C3.1. Gateway Medical Waste Transport of Colorado, Inc.

Financial projections	Year 1	Year 2	Year 3
Estimated sales revenue	$511,000.00	$880,000.00	$1,303,500.00
Estimated costs of goods sold	204,000.00	348,000.00	515,000.00
Estimated gross margin	307,000.00	532,000.00	788,500.00
Variable expenses	13,200.00	13,200.00	14,000.00
Utilities/communications	3,600.00	4,000.00	5,000.00
Office expense	2,500.00	3,000.00	4,000.00
Auto expense	1,200.00	1,500.00	2,000.00
Fuel	8,700.00	10,000.00	15,000.00
Repairs and maintenance	2,000.00	2,000.00	5,000.00
Marketing/advertising	6,000.00	6,000.00	6,000.00
Accounting/legal	1,200.00	1,500.00	1,500.00
Miscellaneous	1,200.00	1,500.00	2,000.00
Total variable expenses	39,600.00	42,700.00	54,500.00
Margin for fixed expenses and net income	267,400.00	489,300.00	734,000.00
Fixed expenses			
Salaries	130,000.00	150,000.00	200,000.00
Rent	14,700.00	14,700.00	20,000.00
Taxes	12,200.00	13,000.00	15,000.00
Loan payments	20,400.00	22,000.00	30,000.00
General liability insurance	11,616.00	13,000.00	20,000.00
Worker's compensation	10,800.00	12,000.00	20,000.00
Medical/life insurance	4,800.00	6,000.00	10,000.00
Unemployment, federal/state	3,000.00	4,000.00	10,000.00
Total fixed expenses	207,516.00	234,700.00	325,000.00
Estimated net income before taxes	59,884.00	254,600.00	409,000.00
Estimated income taxes	11,977.00	76,380.00	159,510.00
Estimated net income after taxes	47,907.00	178,220.00	249,490.00
Estimated income earnings per share (100,000 shares)	0.48	1.78	2.50

Case 4

National Foundations, Inc.

Robert E. Stevens
David L. Loudon
Bruce E. Winston

Kent Smith sits at his desk reviewing his notes on a new product that his company is considering adding. The product, a foundation stabilizing system, could dramatically change the company's product line and growth potential.

Bill and Kent Smith established National Foundations, Inc., in 1978 as a residential foundation repair company. Both brothers worked in another foundation repair company before starting their own business. National Foundations specializes in repair of residential foundations and does no commercial jobs. The need for foundation repair arises when a foundation—usually a concrete slab—settles due to shifting soils, expansion or contraction of soils, or inadequate construction of the original foundation. Repairs normally consist of digging under the existing foundation, jacking the foundation back into position with hydraulic jacks, and then pouring new concrete under the foundation. Cosmetic repair of bricks, shrubs, and grass may also be needed to restore the home to an acceptable condition after repair.

The new product under consideration involves the use of a "seep hose" which can be tied to a home's water system to maintain the moisture content of the soil under a foundation. When the moisture content of the soil decreases, the seep hose would replace the moisture to maintain a constant level. The constant moisture content of the soil would conceivably prevent the soil from expanding or contracting when long dry spells or extremely wet spells occurred, thus, preventing foundation problems. However, the founder and patent holder, Dr. Harold Jenkins, had not completed any field-testing of the product.

Consumer Analysis

Smith realized that the need for residential foundation repairs and/ or preventive systems is based on two factors: (1) the number of structures existing at a given point in time, and (2) the proportion of these structures experiencing foundation failures of sufficient magnitude to warrant repair. He also knew that the number of existing structures is influenced by population, family formations, income levels, and interest rates; while the proportion of structures needing repairs or preventive systems is determined by bearing soil and climatic conditions and/or inadequate foundation construction. Kent understood that he needed to check each of these factors for reliability before he could estimate the sales volume of the new product.

Residential Housing in the United States

Using the U. S. Census housing data, Smith found that the number of existing residential houses in the United States was 109,800,000 units. Growth in housing units, as measured by new housing starts, has followed the pattern shown in Tables C4.1 and C4.2.

TABLE C4.1. Percent of homes by year built.

Year Range	Percent of Homes Built
1990-1994	6
1985-1989	8
1980-1984	8
1975-1979	11
1970-1974	11
1960-1969	15
1950-1959	13
1940-1949	8
1930-1939	6
1920-1929	5
1919-earlier	9
Total	100

TABLE C4.2. New housing starts by year (in thousands).

Year	Number
1992	1,200
1993	1,228
1994	1,457
1995	1,354
1996	1,477
1997	1,476

Source: National Association of Home Builders (NAHB) housing starts, available online at http://www.nahb.com/starts.html.

More relevant to National's planning was the number of homes in the areas most likely to experience the soil and climatic conditions that cause foundation failures. In the continental United States seventeen states have been labeled "problem states" as far as foundation failures are concerned. These states are listed in Table C4.3 along with the number of existing houses in 1999.

Smith planned to use these data to calculate market potential for the sales of the foundation stabilization system in the seventeen problem states. He learned that an estimated 60 percent of all houses built on expansive soils will experience foundation problems of some type. Ten percent of these are estimated to experience problems significant enough to warrant repair. Smith thought that, perhaps, 70 percent of the houses in the seventeen problem states were built on expansive soils.

Market Potential

Table C4.3 shows the total number of houses in each of the seventeen problem states. These data would serve as a basis for estimating total market potential in these states. Table C4.4, in turn, shows the total number of houses for the four cities in which National would initially do business.

TABLE C4.3. Housing in the seventeen problem states, 1999.

State	Number of houses (in thousands)
Alabama	1,834
California	11,599
Colorado	1,493
Florida	5,474
Kansas	1,194
Mississippi	1,140
Montana	410
Nebraska	781
New Mexico	635
North Dakota	324
Oklahoma	1,546
Oregon	1,354
South Dakota	346
Texas	6,936
Utah	613
Washington	2,111
Wyoming	235
Total	38,025

Source: Robert Wade Brown, *Residential Foundations: Design, Behavior, and Repair,* Second Edition. New York: VanNostrand Reinhold, 1984, p. 18.

TABLE C4.4. Housing in four selected cities.

City	Number of houses (in thousands)
Tulsa	195
Oklahoma City	221
Dallas	488
Fort Worth	195
Total	1,099

Consumer and Builder Input

The Smith brothers realized that before they could make a decision on their new venture, they needed to know what home owners and builders thought about foundation problems and repairs. Consequently, they spent many hours interviewing respondents from both groups.

The consumer interviews involved a random sample of home owners in the Tulsa area. The Smiths talked with fifty respondents from a group of home owners who had experienced foundation problems and repairs. This information was used to more precisely estimate repair costs, market share, and interest in the foundation stabilizing system under consideration.

Kent Smith summarized the findings from the home owner survey as follows: of the fifty respondents, frame (wood) (32.3 percent), all brick (31.3 percent), and brick and frame (23.2 percent) were the most popular types of homes. Of the ten respondents who were extremely interested in the system, half (five) had all-brick homes with only one individual with a wood-frame home. Brick homes that show exterior cracks are the prime target for such a system.

- Although the homes with crawl spaces (53.7 percent) outnumbered the homes with slabs (43.2 percent), twice as many individuals who were extremely interested in the system had slab foundations.
- The majority of the homes in the survey were 2,000 square feet or less. None of the respondents with 3,000 square feet or more were interested in the system. This is not to say that those individuals with large homes are not interested in such a system. Larger homes may be perceived as better constructed and thus not in need of the system. Interest in the stabilizing system did increase if respondents were aware of problems in their neighborhood. Of those aware of the problems, 44.4 percent said they were extremely interested in the system. This compares with only 6.6 percent who were not aware of problems.
- Those who experienced foundation problems were not more interested in the system than those who had not. The stabilization system may be viewed as either preventing foundation problems for those who have not had problems or as a stabilization system for those who have experienced problems.

- Of the respondents who experienced foundation problems, 77.8 percent listed foundation settling as the primary type of problem. Exterior cracks were the usual indication of problems. Only 55.6 percent of the respondents had repaired their foundation. The average cost was less than $2,500. Most individuals making repairs spend only a minimal amount while a few must make major costly repairs. Thus, the average cost of repairs is expected to be much greater than just $2,500.
- Of those who were extremely interested in the system and responded to the question on what they expect to pay for the system, more than half responded with greater than $5,000. Thus, for those extremely interested, the present cost of $4,000 does not seem unreasonable.
- When asked if they were still interested if the system costs $4,000, 60 percent responded that they were still extremely interested.
- Of those extremely interested in the system, 50 percent said that they would prefer to pay over time; 71.4 percent of those that were only somewhat interested in the system were interested in paying over time. The availability of credit appeared to be important in marketing the system.
- Of those extremely interested in the system, all were married, and of those 90 percent had children at home. No singles or marrieds without children were extremely interested in the system.
- The primary age category extremely interested in the system was thirty-five to forty-four years old. Of the individuals in this age category, 20.83 percent said they were extremely interested in this system. The next interested age categories were the twenty-five to thirty-four and fifty-five to sixty-four age categories with a combined 15.4 percent.
- Educational levels did not differentiate interest in the system. Those with higher levels of education were slightly less likely to be interested.
- Of those who said that they had experienced foundation problems, 55.6 percent had all-brick homes. Again, these respondents were likely to have noticed exterior cracks. Respondents with other types of homes may have experienced foundation problems but were unaware of them.

- Most of the homes with foundation problems (88.9 percent) had a market value of less than $85,000. More expensive homes may be constructed in such a way as to minimize foundation problems.
- Those likely to purchase the system usually made more purchases than planned compared to those not likely to purchase the system. Thus, the ten individuals who said they were extremely interested in the system may be acting on impulse and may not purchase the system when offered.

Interviews with ten home builders from the area provided insight into their interest in the system. Table C4.5 summarizes the results.

Financial Considerations

The stabilization system is estimated to cost an average of $3,650 per installation. A cost breakdown is shown in Table C4.6.

An engineering report, provided by a civil engineering firm on a fee-for-service basis, along with soil samples, determines the depth at which to install the system for maximum foundation stabilization. The average price per installation is expected to be about $4,500 yielding a 19 percent markup or a contribution-per-installation of $850. Since many consumers were expected to want to finance the system over at least five years, a local bank agreed to finance creditworthy home owners.

Although the addition of the stabilization system was seen as a complementary product to the repair business, Smith anticipated a substantial investment in materials, crew training, and equipment. In addition, the firm would need to locate additional capital as new areas were developed. Estimates of the initial investment needed for each market area are $150,000. This includes all the expenses of opening a new branch office; leasing office and storage space; hiring a general manager, sales staff, secretary, and work crews; equipment rentals; purchase of tools; and working capital of $25,000 per branch.

Since the firm was already in business in Tulsa, the initial investment was expected to be only about $50,000 for that market. However, since the concept of a stabilization system was new, promotion expenses were expected to run about $50,000 a year for the first three

TABLE C4.5. Home builders' survey.

Name	Home value	Comments
Mike Freeze Mike Freeze, Inc.	$65,000 to $85,000	Uses home owner's warranty (HOW) and does not see benefit of foundation stabilization system.
Larry Ogden Ogden Properties	$90,000 to $250,000	System is a good idea and he is interested in concept.
Dave Millsap Dave Millsap, Inc.	$150,000 to $400,000	Had a bad experience with the system on five different occasions. He indicates that system does not work and that it cannot be properly maintained.
Bill Hood Timberwood Custom Homes	$160,000 to $400,000	He is not interested in the system. He indicated that if foundation were put in properly you would not have problems. Get a soil test before building to determine soil type. He does not believe system works on some soils that do not need moisture.
William Howard Timbercrest	$55,000 to $90,000	He feels the same as previous respondent.
Perry Cox, President Cox Properties	$50,000 to $90,000	He feels the same as previous respondent.
Boyd Preston Prestige Homes	Over $120,000	He may be interested for higher-priced homes of $250,000 or more.
Leonard Frye Frye Homes	Over $200,000	He may be interested if building in an area with unstable soil.
Jim Glenn Glenn Homes	$150,000 to $400,000	He thinks the system is a good idea and is needed. He uses french drains on most homes.
Gary Smith Smith Homes, Inc.	$70,000 to $150,000	Every home is piered, which he believes will solve the problem.

TABLE C4.6. Cost per installation.

Item	Cost
Material	$1,800
Labor	$1,200
Engineering report	$200
Sales commissions	$450
Total	$3,650

years of operation and at least $25,000 to $30,000 a year thereafter for all locations.

Additional crews could be added and equipment rented within a short period of time to allow for wide variations in demand for the system. In the Tulsa market, a 2 to 5 percent penetration would yield a substantial base from which to expand into other areas of the country.

The Smiths needed to calculate the expected returns they would make from an investment in the foundation system. In a proposed venture, the net inflows of cash expected from a project should be equal to or greater than the net profit after taxes plus depreciation. The analysis should terminate after ten years with zero salvage at that time, which would force the new company to stand alone with only the near-term cash flows determining operational feasibility. The company wanted the new venture to generate an internal rate of return of at least 15 percent if it were to be launched.

Case 5

Mildred's Caddy

Robert E. Stevens
David L. Loudon
Bruce E. Winston

Mildred Sanders was trying to decide what she should do about her latest invention—an ironing board caddy. Mildred is an entrepreneur at heart, although she spends most of her work time in a real estate firm in Jackson, Mississippi, in which she is a partner. Mildred's creative energies, though, always seemed to focus on new products. She already received a patent on a previous invention as well as the new Ironing Board Caddy (see Figures C5.1 and C5.2).

The Ironing Board Caddy is a clip-on attachment that holds a bottle of spray starch or sizing, scissors, safety pins, and needles and thread. This device prevents items from falling off the ironing board, and if needed, permits the user to repair a garment while ironing.

Mildred asked a friend who did marketing research to help her design a questionnaire to collect data from consumers to estimate acceptance of the product idea. Mildred's friend hired two people to conduct 100 telephone interviews in Jackson using a random sample of potential consumers. In addition, Mildred's friend collected secondary data on households in several southern states. Mildred felt the results of the consumer survey were favorable and that the prospect for sales at very low levels of penetration could produce a substantial profit potential.

Mildred obtained production estimates from three possible manufacturers. These cost estimates ranged from $2.35 to $2.45 per unit in

Names, selected data, and corporate identities have been disguised.

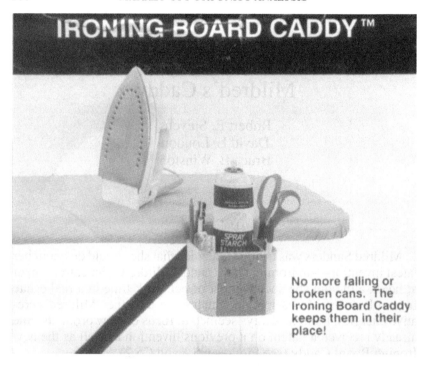

FIGURE C5.1. Mildred's Ironing Board Caddy.

lots of 5,000 or more. Packaging costs were expected to be about 40¢ per unit. The manufacturer selected would require an injection mold for the product that would cost $26,500. Mildred located a reputable package design firm and secured an estimate of $3,500 for a final design. Each of the three manufacturers agreed to store and ship the units in cases of 24 at an additional cost of .10 per unit or $2.40 per case.

At a wholesale price of $6.50, a retailer could sell the product for $12.95 and make a profit of about 50 percent. This markup would make the product fairly attractive if a large volume was sold. To obtain retail distribution, Mildred could use manufacturers' reps. Reps require a 15 percent commission on new products. These reps could also reach fabric/sewing outlets—a key channel in Mildred's thinking.

A regional promotional campaign to launch the product was expected to cost between $75,000 and $100,000 if newspaper inserts and direct mail promotion were used. Mildred was not sure how she could reach potential users more directly.

As a first step in assessing market potential for the Southeastern United States, Mildred's marketing research friend gathered data on the number of households in twelve Southeastern states. This information is shown in Table C5.1.

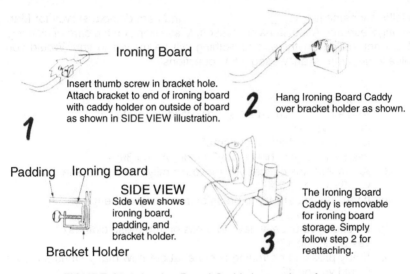

FIGURE C5.2. Ironing Board Caddy instructions for use.

TABLE C5.1. Number of households in the Southeastern United States.

State	Number (in thousands)	State	Number (in thousands)
Alabama	1,342	Arkansas	816
Florida	3,744	Georgia	1,872
Kentucky	1,263	Louisiana	1,412
Mississippi	827	N. Carolina	2,043
S. Carolina	1,030	Tennessee	1,619
Virginia	4,452	W. Virginia	1,705

Source: U.S. Bureau of the Census.

Mildred then sought to identify characteristics of potential consumers through the questionnaire shown in Figure C5.3. This questionnaire produced data on (1) marital status, (2) family composition, (3) incidence of ironing, (4) spray starch/sizing usage, (5) problems related to functions performed on the ironing board, and (6) reactions to features/price of the proposed new product.

Hello, my name is _____, and I am doing a survey for Marketing Research Associates in Jackson, Mississippi, on the care of clothing. I am not selling anything, and nothing will be mailed to you. Would you please help me by answering a few questions?

1. First, are you
   single 8%   married 78%   divorced/separated 7%
   or widowed 7%
2. Do you have children at home?
   yes 61%   If yes, how many? mode=2   no 39%
3. Are most of the clothes you (or your family) wear permanent press?
   yes 85%   no 15%
4a. If yes, do you still try to press or iron many of them?
   yes 97%   no 3%
4b. If no, do you usually have to press or iron these clothes?
   yes 83%   no 17%
5. If any pressing or ironing is done, about how many times a month would you do it?
   1-2 16%   3-4 26%   5-6 12%   7-8 1%   9-10 9%   over 10 36%
6. Do you use an ironing board?
   yes 98%   no 2%
7. Do you use spray starch or sizing?
   yes 70%   no 30%
8. If yes, about how many cans of starch/sizing would you use in a year?
   1-3 40%   4-6 22%   7-9 3%   10-12 10%   13-15 3%   16-18 3%
   19 or more 19%
9. Do you ever do mending, sewing, or altering on the ironing board?
   yes 64%   no 36%
10. If yes, do you ever experience problems of:
    a. starch/sizing can falls off the ironing board? 77% yes
    b. no convenient place to keep pins, scissors, etc., close to your ironing board? 72% yes

FIGURE C5.3. Market potential survey for Ironing Board Caddy.

11. If an inexpensive product were on the market that held your spray starch, scissors, pins, etc., and would attach to your ironing board, would you buy it?

    yes <u>56%</u> no <u>21%</u> maybe <u>19%</u> don't know <u>4%</u>

12. How much would you expect to pay for such a product?

    $8.00 or less <u>0%</u> $10.01 to 11.00 <u>1%</u>
    $8.01 to 9.00 <u>16%</u> $11.01 to 12.00 <u>2%</u>
    $9.01 to 10.00 <u>45%</u>   over $12.00 <u>36%</u>

Thank you very much for your help.

FIGURE C5.3 *(continued)*

TABLE C5.2. Profile of potential buyers based on Jackson Market Study.

Characteristic profile*	Answers
Marital status	78% married
Children at home	61% children at home
Type of clothing	85% most are permanent press
Pressing of clothes	97% press clothes
Frequency of pressing	5-6 times per month
Use of ironing board	98% use ironing board
Use of spray starch/sizing	70% use spray starch/sizing
Problems—can falling off	77% experienced this problem
Problems—no place for pins, etc.	72% experienced this problem
Expected price	$9.75 median price expected

*The values shown are for those respondents who said they would purchase the product if available.

By cross-tabulating the responses to the questions, it was possible to develop a profile of the potential purchasers of the caddy. Table C5.2 shows the profile derived from the respondents who said yes to the question about buying the product. Mildred thought these characteristics pointed to clearly identifiable market segments interested in this product.

Mildred estimated that she would need a minimum capital investment of about $132,200 to launch the product if she decided to market the product herself. This included $75,000 for a regional promotional campaign, $12,200 for production of the first 5,000 units, $26,500 for the injection mold, $3,500 for package design, and another $15,000 to cover packaging and administrative costs. She knew she had access to that amount because of her real estate holdings but wondered if she should risk it in the venture or simply try to license another company to manufacture and market the product.

Mildred knew she would only get about 10 percent per unit under a licensing arrangement but that the manufacturer would assume the risk of the venture. She also wondered what would be involved in a thorough and complete marketing strategy for the ironing board caddy if she were to implement it herself and not license the product. Production and marketing of a previous product idea had produced disappointing results. She also knew she needed to decide soon before someone else came up with a similar idea and she also wanted to get back the $9,500 she had already spent in getting the product patented.

Case 6

Jay's Travel Trailer Park

Robert E. Stevens
David L. Loudon
Bruce E. Winston

Jay Fenton had just completed his first year in the travel trailer park business. The purchase of the park a year earlier was Jay's "retirement" investment. The $300,000 purchase price seemed to be a way to invest some of his retirement funds in an area close to relatives but still provide an attractive annual income.

The thirty-nine-unit park was located off a main highway leading to a lake in one of the state's most beautiful and biggest resort areas. The park contained an office, swimming pool, laundry room, restrooms, sanitary dump, and picnic areas. In addition, the park had the potential to add more trailer sites with water and electrical hookups. The park was located on the corner of a forty-acre plot, leaving plenty of room for expansion. Although there was no current access to a creek that bordered the property, there was potential for developing beach and boat access to the creek as well as other attractions.

The lackluster performance of the park caused Jay to consider other options. One possibility was to invest more money in park development and promotion to create a "destination park" rather than the current "pass-through" park orientation. Destination parks were developed with more amenities and guests averaged longer stays, while pass-through parks offered minimum amenities and were designed for guests en route to another destination. In searching for some answers, Jay obtained data on parks and camping from the state's tourism department.

Tourism and Recreation

The state has developed and supported a great deal of tourist and recreationally oriented attractions during the past decade. The development of a lake and dam gave impetus to more rapid development of this area.

The Northwest area is the second-ranked area in the state for overnight visitors. Of the total 24,107,500 overnight visitors to the state last year, about 22 percent were in the Northwest area (see Table C6.1).

Smith County attracts the greatest number of overnight visitors. Although Washington County is far behind as a destination, it leads the entire region as the economic and population center. As such, Washington County could be a source of weekend business during the slow seasons.

Overnight Campers

Overnight campers represent a specific segment of the tourism market. They accounted for about 7.2 percent of the state's overnight visitors last year (see Table C6.2).

More pertinent to this overnight segment is the number of group nights (shown in Table C6.3), which is the total number of parties (three to four people) times the number of nights' stay in a particular area. Table C6.3 shows the actual nights in total for the state and then estimated nights for the northwest area.

These two tables together show that last year, for example, 97,904 camping parties came to the area, stayed an average of 7.6 days, and

TABLE C6.1. Overnight visitors in the Northwest area.

County	Visitors	State Share (in Percent)
Smith	2,543,340	10.55
Rankin	2,143,155	8.89
Simpson	26,515	0.11
Washington	605,100	2.51
Total	5,318,110	22.06

TABLE C6.2. Camping activity for the past three years.

	Two Years Ago	One Year Ago	Last Year
Overnight campers	1,788,700	1,885,470	1,730,900
Parties	506,030	496,175	443,810
Average stay (nights)	7.4	6.8	7.6
Persons per party	3.6	3.8	3.9
Person-night	13,236,380	12,821,196	13,154,840
Spent per party-night	$31.45	$33.87	$35.97
Annual economic impact	$117,768,360	$114,277,040	$121,325,220
Percent by category			
Truck-camp	33.5%	32.0%	32.5%
RV-camp	49.6%	50.0%	49.0%
Tent-camp	16.9%	18.0%	18.5%
Total	100.0%	100.0%	100.0%
Trip nights	3,744,622	3,373,990	3,372,956

TABLE C6.3. Camper party nights: State and Northwest region.

	State			Northwest Region		
	Two years ago	One year ago	Last year	Two years ago	One year ago	Last year
Parties	506,030	496,175	443,810	103,129	109,010	97,904
Avg. stay	7.4	6.8	7.6	7.4	6.8	7.6
Group nights	3,744,622	3,373,990	3,372,956	763,155	741,268	744,070

used 3,641,594 RV campsites and 137,653 tent campsites. The area's share of campers is 63 percent of all overnight visitors, and that the percentage of campers by type is basically the same in the Northwest area as for the state as a whole.

Competitive Analysis

Jay found that three basic marketing strategies are used by private trailer park facilities. One strategy is aimed at the overnight or pass-through market. These parks are designed to appeal to travelers en route to some predetermined destination or those who are in a location for a short (one- to three-day) period. These parks are usually close to major highways and offer few amenities to guests.

A second strategy is aimed at those travelers who are planning an extended stay (four to seven days) in a particular area—usually a resort or other major tourist attraction. Although these trailer parks do not contain many amenities, they are located very close to if not adjacent to the attraction.

A third strategy is geared toward the extended traveler, and includes all, or most, of the amenities in the park itself. Thus the park becomes the attraction and offers facilities and services geared to guests who will remain in the area for a few days.

Jay's research of competitors revealed that all three strategies existed in the Northwest area of the state. The major competitors in the Washington-Smith County area are shown in Table C6.4. This table clearly demonstrates the differences in services offered in this area. Yogi Bear's Jellystone Park is by far the most complete—using the concept of a self-contained resort; it offers the full range of services. KOA and Safari basically use the same strategy but with fewer amenities. KOA's location on a major state highway also appeals to overnighters. Safari is being expanded at the present time to offer more sites and amenities.

Jay's Travel Trailer Park uses the strategy of not providing amenities but locating close to them. It is within a mile of the Corps of Engineers Recreational Area. The park offers nothing more than a place to park a trailer; however, a grocery store, boats, bait, picnic tables, and other amenities are all close to the park. A couple of mobile home parks in the area offer overnight hookups but cater strictly to overnighters and probably the overflow of other RV parks.

A new proposed park located only 100 yards off a major highway is planned and is awaiting a zoning decision. Judging from the location and amount of land used in development, it would appear to be aimed at the pass-through or short-stay market.

TABLE C6.4. RV trailer parks by type of amenities.

RV trailer park	Coffee snack bar	Group shelter	Restrooms	Laundry room	Swimming pool	Sanitary dump	Showers	Picnic tables	Rec. room	Boats	Teen hut	Planned activities	All hook-ups	Tennis courts	Barbecue grill	Tent area	Playground	Number of units
KOA	X		X	X	X	X	X	X	X				X			X	X	60
Yogi Bear's Jellystone Park	X	X	X	X	X	X	X	X	X	X	X	X	X	X	X	X		60
Safari	X		X	X	X	X	X		X					X	X			24
Jay's Travel Trailer Park			X	X	X	X		X					X					39
Karl's Mobile Home Park					X			X										10

189

The real opportunities in the RV park business appear to be destination parks. These parks are close to major population centers (up to four hours driving time) and offer urban RV owners a chance for fun on weekends and vacations.

Destination parks require a major financial commitment because they offer many activities to keep guests busy. A typical list of activities and related facilities includes: swimming, fishing, and boating; golf (including miniature golf); children's playgrounds; horses; jet skis; waterskiing; separate recreational buildings for adults and youths; tennis; hayrides; picnic areas; Ping-Pong; shuffleboard; horseshoes; archery; hiking and bicycle trails; restaurants/bars; general store; laundries; movies; etc. Most important is a planned recreation program for children, teenagers, and adults. Such parks earn about half of their revenue from fees other than for space. The goal is fun, fun, fun for everybody, so that visitors stay longer and return frequently.

A second category of destination parks requires less investment in facilities but usually much higher costs for land. Located near a major attraction, such as Disney World, visitors to such parks are attracted by fun and sightseeing activities in the surrounding area.

RV park rates are rising rapidly, however, this has not affected RV travel; it is still more economical than other modes of travel.

Although the rate of return for a successful RV park investment is higher than for a mobile home park, the risk is much greater. Feasibility studies for RV parks are more subject to error; in contrast, such studies for mobile home parks are almost foolproof. One problem with RV park investments is that mortgage money is more difficult to obtain. The financial community is aware of the successful record for mobile home parks. RV parks are much newer and have no well-established financial record.

As Jay considered his options, he also reflected on the need for an effective marketing strategy. One consistent observation he made of private, nonfranchised trailer parks is that they lacked an effective marketing program. Thus, he realized that the marketing activities would be part of the overall effective management of the park.

Target Market

Although Jay carefully identified several potential market segments, he was not sure which of these he should target. The segments included the following:

1. *Cross-country travelers* en route to a predetermined destination looking strictly for overnight hookups.
2. *Cross-country travelers* en route to a specific area of the country but with no definite destination in mind—looking for some overnight and some short-stay (two to four days) accommodations.
3. *Local area residents,* usually weekenders, on short trips with a predetermined destination—tourist attractions, horse shows, lake recreation area, etc. They mostly want overnight hookups but also need some short-stay accommodations.
4. *RV clubs, large multiunit family groups, sport spectators* may be local area residents and/or nonlocal residents, depending on the nature of the group involved. They may want only overnight accommodations for a short stay.

Jay knew that the marketing mix (consisting of location, amenities, price, and promotion) should be put together with a specific group in mind. For example, a strictly overnight park would be located close to a major highway, offer few amenities, and not require a park theme. Figure C6.1 shows some of the possible positions available for a new or redesigned park attempting to "fit in" with existing offerings.

The current trend in travel trailer parks is in the direction of the high amenity concept such as Yogi Bear's Jellystone Park. These parks appeal to the extended-stay market (five to seven days) with a complete array of amenities from laundry rooms to planned activities for children. At the other end of the scale are mobile home parks, which have a few sites for travel trailers and offer no specific amenities.

Low Amenities				High Amenities
Karl's Mobile Home Park	Jay's Travel Trailer Park	KOA	Safari	Yogi Bear's Jellystone Park

FIGURE C6.1. Positioning a trailer park.

Price

The prices charged by different trailer parks reflect three things: (1) competition, (2) amenities offered, and (3) usage or costs associated with serving guests. More amenities mean a higher price. Typical prices for RV parks reflect these factors and are shown in Table C6.5.

This price structure reflects current competitive prices for a park with several amenities. Jay's Travel Trailer Park currently offers few amenities and charges a flat rate of $10.50 per night.

Using current revenue and expense data, Jay knew he could estimate revenue and expenses for expansion to a 100-site destination-type park for average occupancy levels. The park had a 45 percent occupancy rate last year, and Jay felt that repositioning the park as a 100-site destination park would increase occupancy rates to at least 65 percent. If expansion was feasible, Jay knew he would still need an effective marketing plan to increase occupancy.

Jay estimated that an additional $1,110,000 would be needed for expansion of the park and to reposition it close to Yogi Bear's Jellystone Park. This included sixty-one more sites, additional pools, a waterslide, access to the river, a canoe rental shop, a riding stable, driving range, and other amenities needed to reposition the park as a destination park. (See Table C6.6 for income statement information.)

A less aggressive strategy would be to add some amenities and position the park close to the KOA-Safari position. Jay felt that this would result in a 55 percent occupancy rate and would require an investment of $500,000. Table C6.7 offers a breakdown of the cost estimates for adding additional amenities.

Jay was still undecided about what he should do next. He knew he could not continue the current losses but wondered if a more effective promotional campaign might increase occupancy without any additional capital investment.

TABLE C6.5. Typical RV park's services and rates.

Amenities	Price per Night
All hookups (two people)	$19.95
Water or electricity only	$15.50
No hookups	$10.50
Charge for each additional person	$1.00
Air conditioner or heater surcharge	$5.00

Table C6.6. Last year's income statement.

Income and Expenses	Dollars
Occupancy, based on seven-month season (210 days)	45%
No. of spaces rented	3,686
Gross income	$38,703
Extra occupancy	2,126
Vending machines, laundry	2,835
Store sales	28,350
Total Income	$72,014
Less cost of goods sold	27,010
Gross profit	$45,004
Less expenses	
Salaries	$10,500
Payroll taxes	1,994
Property taxes	2,723
Insurance	2,160
Advertising and signs	3,000
Office expense and supplies	300
Telephone	600
Electricity	3,835
Water	1,834
Maintenance—bldg. and ground, trash	200
Maintenance—pool	1,000
Maintenance—roads	300
Depreciation	9,226
All other expenses	2,500
Total expenses	$40,172
Income before debt service and taxes	$4,832
Interest expense	12,000
Taxes	0
Profit	($7,168)

TABLE C6.7. Amenity cost estimates.

Amenity	Cost
Land preparation/landscaping	$180,000
Site preparation (61)	61,000
Paving roads	250,000
Drainage/sewage	75,000
Large pool (40' x 80')	38,000
Small pool (25' x 60')	33,000
Recreation building (adult)	125,000
Recreation building (youth)	112,000
Waterslide	30,000
River access	25,000
Canoes/rental building	15,000
Concession stands (2)	6,000
Stable and horses	15,000
Driving range	25,000
Miniature golf course	25,000
Equipment	30,000
Miscellaneous supplies	15,000
Additional working capital	50,000
Total additional capital	$1,110,000

Case 7

The Box Factory, Inc.

Robert E. Stevens
David L. Loudon

Charles Smith was wondering what his next move should be in developing the market for his die-cast toy car display case. He knew he had to use a cost-effective marketing strategy based on his limited financial resources. He did not feel he had developed his ideas well enough to secure a bank loan or to interest potential investors, but he knew he had a product with good potential sales if he could just get it launched. He was even more encouraged when a friend showed him all the Web sites related to collecting die-cast toy cars and trucks and the widespread interest in these collectibles.

Background

Charles and Cindy Smith incorporated The Box Factory in 1994, for the purpose of making and selling woodwork crafts. The Box Factory developed a product for the storage and display of die-cast toy cars. The basic design of this product is a wooden shadow box in the form of an eighteen-wheeler truck (see Figure C7.1). Encouraged by friends and relatives, the Smiths set up a mail-order system for consumers to purchase the product. The Box Factory advertised the display case in *Country Sampler* magazine in April 1994. Response to the advertisement was overwhelming, so the Smiths decided to keep concentrating on mail-order sales. The success of the wooden product prompted The Box Factory to research producing the truck in plastic and distributing it through retail outlets. A patent was obtained for the plastic display case.

To act as an agent for the production and sale of the plastic product, The Box Factory entered into an agreement with a design company.

FIGURE C7.1. The wooden display unit.

A prototype of a plastic, injection-molded truck was developed and displayed at a convention in 1995. At this time, a major toy manufacturer requested a proposal on licensing the product from the design company. The design company responded to The Box Factory with a new agent agreement that drastically increased the design company's commissions. The Smiths refused to sign the new agreement and all communication with the design company ceased. Since that time, no further attempts to commercialize the product have taken place.

The contract established with the design company expired in August 1997, thus releasing The Box Factory from any obligations. This created the opportunity for The Box Factory to enter the market with the plastic, injection-molded, wall-mounted display case for die-cast toy cars. Die-cast toy cars considered to be collectibles ranged in price from 99¢ to $99.

Market Analysis

Collecting stamps, baseball cards, or bottle caps has always been a favorite pastime; this does not differ in the case of die-cast toy cars. Many people collect Hot Wheels and Matchbox brand cars; as with most collectors, these individuals want to showcase their collections.

Customers of The Box Factory, Inc., are mainly adults. Men mostly collect Hot Wheels and Matchbox cars, while women tend to buy them as gifts for collectors or for their children. The Internet contains numerous Web sites devoted to the collection of Hot Wheels and Matchbox toy cars. These data reinforce the belief that a market for The Box Factory's product exists.

Parents will buy the product to fulfill two purposes: first, to provide a place for their children to store the cars when they are not playing with them, and, second, as a way to decorate their children's rooms. Collectors need a place to store their cars, showcase their prized collectibles, and organize their collections.

Since the majority of the purchases are gifts, sales for the wooden display case typically increase during the months between October and January (due in large part to Christmas). Women make the majority of the purchases of the display cases, and men make most of the individual toy car purchases.

Product Analysis

A wooden version of the mounted display case enjoyed a great deal of sales success in the years leading up to this point. Advertising in only one hobby magazine produced sales of over $50,000 in the first year. These magazine ads generated sales for five years, with a number of sales occurring after the ads were cut at the beginning of 1996. The sales of the wooden display case provided evidence that a market for this type of product existed. Table C7.1 shows the sales of the wooden display case; however, promotions for this product were cut in 1996.

The new product would be an injection-molded, wall-mounted display case designed to house twenty die-cast cars (Hot Wheels and Matchbox cars). The case is fashioned in the design of an eighteen-wheeler truck; it is 28 inches long, 8 1/2 inches high, and 3/4 inches deep. The estimated production cost per unit is $3.50.

The product would be shipped in a protective cardboard box, the same type of package used by the Box Factory to send the wooden display cases to its customers. This package costs approximately 40¢ per unit.

TABLE C7.1. Sales by year.

Year	Sales (in dollars)
April 1991 to December 1993	200,000
January 1994 to December 1994	60,000
January 1995 to June 1995	20,000
July 1995 to December 1996	20,000

The two target markets identified by the Smiths (collectors and children) complicate the product decision. In order for the same product design to relate to different market segments with such vast distinctions, the product must differ in some way. One inexpensive means of changing the product might be accomplished by varying the color. For the product to appeal to the collectors' market segment, a wood finish appearance could be used. The children's segment could implement a more "playful" image with red, blue, and yellow to better relate to this target market.

Competitive Analysis

Presently, there was no direct competition for The Box Factory's mounted display case. However, a few similar products could pose a threat. A handful of companies produce plastic display cases designed and marketed to display much larger cars. These cases could be used to showcase seven to ten die-cast cars; however, they do not have any eye-catching features. They are made up of plastic bases and clear plastic detachable domelike boxes. Some companies also produce these cases to mount on a wall. Another possible more direct competitive threat is carrying cases for small die-cast cars. Numerous types of cases are designed to house many die-cast cars yet they are not fashioned to be fixed display cases. Rather, they are designed to transport or store the toy cars. Table C7.2 shows current competitive cases available and their prices.

TABLE C7.2. Carrying cases and prices.

Product	Price
Hot Wheels Sto & Go (drag race case and playset)	$12.99
Hot Wheels City Playset	6.99
Hot Wheels Sto & Go (parking and service)	14.99
Hot Wheels Sto & Go (super city playset)	14.99
Hot Wheels Cargo Plane	14.99
Hot Wheels Super Rally Case	9.99
Tara Toy 48 Car Case	6.99
Fast Lane (Toy Car Briefcase)	9.99
Garage (Toy Car Storage Case)	5.96

Financial Analysis

The Smiths need to develop an analysis of their break-even point for the plastic display case based on sales of the product directly to consumers as well as through retailers. If the product is sold to retailers, the price would have to provide an adequate markup. Table C7.3 presents the expected cost structure for the Box Factory display case.

The production cost of $3.50 was based on a production run of 5,000 units in one color. At 10,000 units production cost would drop to $2.75 per unit. The company that would produce the plastic unit had a production capacity of 25,000 units a year. The injection model itself would have to be designed and manufactured by a design company. The cost of the mold was estimated to be about $7,500.

The Smiths need to estimate how much additional investment is needed to launch the new product (including the injection mold, purchase of an inventory of shipping boxes, and an investment in inventory of 5,000 display cases) and how much operating capital is needed to cover expenses until the sales volume is high enough to cover operating expenses.

TABLE C7.3. Display case cost structure.

Costs	Per Item
Variable costs	
Production	$3.50
Packaging	$0.40
Shipping (from factory)	$0.50
Comment card and postage	$0.45
Total variable costs	$4.85
Fixed costs	
Storage	$500.00
Salaries	$25,000.00
Advertising	$600.00
Insurance	$250.00
Total fixed costs	$26,350.00

Marketing the New Display Case

The financials for the product indicated that even at sales of 5,000 to 10,000 units, the product could be very profitable. The Smiths' previous marketing approach had been fairly successful for the wooden display case, although they felt they were in the dark about what past customers thought. The Smiths wondered how, in the future, they could obtain feedback from purchasers and exactly what information should be sought to be managerially useful.

The ads they had run produced sales for several years. However, they were not sure about how to reach the children's market or how to get their product into retail stores. The Smiths wondered if there might be a number of children's magazines in which to promote the product or if there were some good specialty magazines carrying unique products that could generate mail orders. They also thought about approaching one of the toy car manufacturers and trying to negotiate a license agreement to manufacture and distribute the display case but were not sure about the implications of such a move.

Their accountant had also suggested contacting one or more major retail chains as possible distributors. The volume that could be generated by any one of these large retailers would probably be enough to handle their current production capacity, especially if they were producing three different colors of the case.

All of these options were evaluated before a decision was made about proceeding with trying to raise the money to launch the new product.

Case 8

Central Bank:
Automatic Teller Machines

Robert E. Stevens
David L. Loudon
Bruce E. Winston

As Mark Chappell, vice president and manager of the Automatic Banking Services department at Central Bank, reviewed the latest month's ATM transaction data and the consumer survey on ATM usage, he wondered about what pricing strategy to recommend to the executive committee. Should he recommend an annual fee for all cardholders, continuation of the current 50¢ fee transaction, or a raise in the current fee to $1 per transaction? The impact of this decision could dramatically affect the bank's earnings and ATM usage.

Background

Automatic teller machines (ATMs) emerged in the early 1970s and have experienced relatively widespread acceptance by both the industry and its customers with many financial institutions aggressively promoting the use of ATMs to their customers. Increasing the base of ATM users can contribute to an institution's profitability in a number of ways. Such transactions can help the institution to (1) stabilize or reduce staff, (2) cut paper processing costs, (3) generate fee income, (4) generate investment funds from high average balance accounts, and (5) reduce labor hours or avoid extending hours. The key to obtaining these benefits is to direct market to those consumers who are most likely to obtain and use an ATM card on a regular basis.

ATMs are extremely important to Central Bank's overall strategy for two reasons: (1) the bank is domiciled in one of the last states to eliminate antibranch banking laws which prohibit a bank from building branches, and (2) studies had shown that the bank's cost per transaction for an ATM was only about 50¢, compared to $1 per transaction with a "live" teller. Since an earlier test case declared that ATMs did not constitute a branch, their proliferation gives banks the opportunity to expand geographically to reach new markets. Central Bank currently has fifteen ATMs in various locations throughout the city with a monthly average of 5,576 transactions per ATM (see Table C8.1). The services offered at each ATM are (1) cash withdrawals, (2) balance inquiries, (3) account transfers, and (4) deposits. The cash withdrawals may be from a checking account, savings account, or credit card. All of the bank's ATMs (except for the one in the bank's main lobby) are "stand-alones," meaning not inside a store but in their own constructed facility. All the ATMs can be accessed twenty-four hours a day, seven days a week. Each ATM is also equipped with a phone for recorded messages on how to use the ATM or what to do if a problem occurs.

TABLE C8.1. Average transactions per machine.

Machine Number	Average Monthly Transactions
1	3,894
2	7,227
3	6,423
4	8,270
5	3,721
6	2,112
7	6,340
8	7,432
9	4,565
10	5,541
11	5,212
12	4,613
13	4,825
14	6,130
15	7,328
Total	83,633

The average use per machine of 5,576 per month was higher than the national average of 4,310. Chappell attributed this to the state antibranch banking laws that prohibited branches prior to 1985. Consumers became more dependent on ATMs to conduct banking transactions and carried on these behavior patterns even after branches were permitted.

The Consumer Study

The bank hired a marketing research firm to study ATM usage in the area to determine reasons for ATM use, services used most, average usage, problems encountered in use, and questions about ATM fees. During a six-week period, the marketing research firm conducted a telephone survey of a random sample of 500 area residents who used the services of a financial institution. The sample is believed to be representative of Central Bank's 10,500 noncommercial clients.

ATM Usage

Tables C8.2 and C8.3 show ATM usage patterns among respondents. Table C8.2 shows that withdrawals and deposits were the two most frequently used functions among study respondents. These figures correspond to national percentages on usage characteristics.

Table C8.3 shows frequency of use among respondents. The first two categories of users were called *active users* based on their frequent use of ATMs. These consumers have altered their banking patterns to include frequent use of ATMs.

TABLE C8.2. Function performed by ATM users.

Function	Percentage*
Deposits	35.6
Withdrawals	77.6
Transfers	3.8
Balance inquiry	3.8
Bill payment	1.0

*Percentages add to more than 100 percent due to respondents giving more than one answer.

TABLE C8.3. Usage frequency.

Frequency of ATM Use	Percentage*
Three or more times per week	26.4
One or two times per week	35.2
Once every two weeks	9.9
Once every three weeks	12.1
Less than once a month	8.8
Don't use anymore	7.7

*Does not add to 100 percent due to rounding.

Price Sensitivity Among Cardholders

Price sensitivity was measured by asking respondents about (1) current card charges, if any, (2) desired transaction charge alternatives—annual fee versus transaction fee, and (3) maximum charge under their choice of fee payment before they would stop using their card. This permitted establishing a method of payment and a level of payment for card usage.

Seventy percent of the respondents reported that they were not currently paying a fee for ATM use. About 17 percent said they were paying a fee, and about 13 percent did not know whether they were paying a fee at the current time.

When respondents were asked their preference for an annual fee or a fee per transaction, 46.3 percent preferred an annual fee, 29.1 percent preferred a fee per transaction, 20.1 percent said they would not use their card if a fee were charged, and 4.5 percent were undecided. Active cardholders showed a stronger preference for an annual fee than inactive cardholders. Only 23.8 percent of the inactive cardholders reported that they would not use their card if the bank charged a fee.

The fee schedules for both the annual fees and the fees per transaction were presented as alternatives by asking if the respondents would be willing to pay a given amount. These results are shown in Tables C8.4 and C8.5. The percentages shown in each column represent the proportion of respondents who were willing to pay a maximum given fee before they would stop using their card.

TABLE C8.4. Alternative fee levels for an annual fee by card ownership.

Maximum Annual Fee	Central Bank %	Non–Central Bank %	Both Combined %	All Cardholders %
Less than $5 a year	4.7	6.1	0.0	5.5
Pay $5 a year	32.6	24.2	9.1	25.3
Pay $10 a year	30.2	33.3	9.1	29.7
Pay $15 a year	9.3	27.3	54.6	20.9
Pay $20 a year	11.6	0.0	18.2	7.7
Pay $30 a year	9.3	0.0	0.0	5.5
Over $30 a year	2.3	9.1	9.1	5.5

TABLE C8. 5. Alternative fee levels for a fee per transaction by card ownership.

Transaction Fee	Central Bank %	Non–Central Bank %	Both Combined %	All Cardholders %
Less than 25¢ per transaction	9.1	18.0	0.0	12.5
Pay 25¢ per transaction	27.3	33.3	66.7	34.7
Pay 50¢ per transaction	45.5	28.2	33.3	31.9
Pay 75¢ per transaction	13.6	7.7	0.0	11.1
Pay $1 per transaction	4.6	10.3	0.0	8.3
Over $1 per transaction	0.0	2.6	0.0	1.4

For those who preferred an annual fee (46.3 percent), almost all (95.4 percent) would be willing to pay $5 a year for the use of their card. For those who preferred a fee per transaction (29.1 percent), at least 90 percent were willing to pay at least 10¢ per transaction to use their card. There were no significant differences between active versus inactive cardholders and all cardholders combined on fee preferences and fee levels.

Awareness of ATMs in the study area was very high overall (94.3 percent), but awareness of specific transactions was concentrated on cash withdrawals and deposits. About 64 percent of the adult population reported owning a card that could be used in an ATM.

Among cardholders, 64.5 percent were classified as active (i.e., they used their card at least once every two weeks). Of the active cardholders, 36.4 percent used their card three times a week and 51.2 percent used their card one to two times a week. The majority of cardholders (68.1 percent) used their cards close to home, on Friday, Saturday, and Sunday, and between 3 p.m. and 10 p.m., which corresponds with the hours banking facilities are traditionally closed.

The overriding motivation for ATM usage was "convenience." Cardholders ranked "overall convenience" more frequently (51.9 percent), than any other reason for getting an ATM card. The second-highest ranking reason was "open twenty-four hours a day" (17.3 percent), which implies convenience and availability.

The Pricing Dilemma

Chappell's review of banking literature revealed three schools of thought about pricing ATM services. The first was not to charge customers at all for ATM use. This was based on the cost savings associated with ATM use compared to "live" tellers. Since financial institutions actually cut costs through ATMs, not charging a service fee should encourage their use.

The second approach was to charge customers for the use of ATM services either with an annual fee (fifteen to twenty dollars per year) or a fee for each transaction (50¢ to $1 per transaction at Central Bank's ATMs). This would create an additional source of revenue for the institution and help recover the cost of ATM installations. (ATM installations ranged from $35,000 for an in-store location to $100,000 plus for a "stand-alone" location.)

A third school of thought, which was gaining popularity among banks, was to provide some free transactions, say three to four per quarter, and then charge for additional transactions on a quarter-by-quarter basis.

Chappell was convinced that the bank should continue to charge for ATM services but wondered if the annual fee might cause nonusers of ATMs to complain or even switch to a competing financial institution.

Case 9

Jill's House of Cakes

Phylis M. Mansfield
Jacquelyn Warwick

Jill sat looking around her kitchen imagining what it would look like twice as big, crowded with people, all making cakes. She had started out baking cakes for friends and family but somewhere along the line it had developed into a small but growing business. She wondered if growing was what she really wanted, and if her neighbors would let her expand her business in her home without complaint. Jill knew she needed to talk to someone with business experience, which was why she had called her friend Debbie, a business consultant, and invited her to lunch. They were to meet in thirty minutes to discuss Jill's future business plans. As she stood and picked up her car keys Jill sighed and mumbled to the empty kitchen, "What am I getting myself into?"

Home Business

Jill had always loved to bake, and her cakes were the talk of every family gathering. It became part of the family tradition to ask what her secret was to making cakes extra light and moist; but Jill, who thought it was flattering to have so many people ask her, would never tell how she accomplished the feat. Family members began to tell their friends who, in turn, started to ask Jill to make cakes for their special family occasions. Before she knew what had happened, she was making ten to fifteen cakes each month. Yet it was not until her best friend from college asked her to send a cake to Connecticut for a very special birthday that Jill found her niche in the market: mail-order cakes. After that, Jill began making three special-order cake packages per day for every major occasion and celebration (such as thank-yous, congratulations, birthdays, anniversaries, Christmas, and Easter) for her friends and shipping them all over the continental United States.

A good share of Jill's business involved making and shipping birthday cakes, which brought in the most consistent cash flow, but not nearly what was needed to buy all the decorating supplies and ingredients for the different holiday seasons that were the biggest times of year for her business. Because of this, capital management was a constant concern since shortages of cash reserves were always a problem.

Even so, Jill's business appeared to be growing quickly in a world where people are all moving at a faster pace and want a gift that can be sent quickly and easily. Since many have moved toward the trend of impersonal, mail-order gift giving, Jill felt that what she provided was the unique opportunity to offer both: a gift sent by mail yet still a "personal" special occasion celebration package. Thus, the uniquely packaged gourmet cake becomes a wonderful alternative to the ever-familiar flowers or candy.

Price

Although Jill had been pricing her cakes at the $20 to $22 level, she was doubtful she could maintain that price with the new cost structure and higher level of competition. When assessing the price of the product, Jill determined she wanted her cakes to be priced below or consistent in price with other gifts that could be delivered to homes. She decided that the delivered cost of the cake should be at the mid- to upper-twenties range (including an 8.5 percent state sales tax and a standard shipping and handling charge for routine orders). To ensure price satisfaction and repeat purchases, Jill often put special party favors or other little treasures unique to the occasion in each box. These inexpensive items would also be included in the cost of the cake.

Distribution

To keep customers satisfied, Jill promised that orders placed before noon would be shipped the same day. This usually worked, although sometimes when people called at 11:30 a.m. it presented a problem. Since 11:30 a.m. was so close to the deadline, if there was any problem in the kitchen the order would often not be sent the same day as promised. Her friends had always been very understanding about this, with the exception of one of her new neighbors, Elizabeth.

A bigger concern was with her delivery service provider. Although she called and stated she needed a refrigeration unit for her shipment, often the driver would come unprepared to pick up her delivery and would need to go back a second time before the cakes could be shipped. However, her husband told her she was worrying over nothing since they did not charge extra for the return trip and the delivery was still sent out on time; so, overall, Jill was happy with her current delivery system.

Competitors

Although her business was growing, Jill constantly worried over the competition in the marketplace. She knew by the number of catalogs she received every day in the mail that there were numerous decisions to consider before current or future customers made the purchase of a gift.

Jill knew that by using accessibility and free delivery as a weapon, local bakeries and gift shops in the area were all current competitors. Indirectly, all the catalogs and florist shops with their toll-free order numbers, as well as national toll-free florists, were potential competitors since they could add gourmet cakes to their product mix and quickly enter the market at any time. As of yet there were no local competitors in the surrounding communities. However, she knew other national companies, which sold cakes through their catalogs, direct-mail pieces, or through their stores, shipped into her area as well as throughout the United States. The constant national advertising campaigns from these large companies were of major concern to Jill since she did not have the same name recognition or money to compete on their level.

Current Operations

When Jill originally made her decision to expand her business, she asked her sister to help her during the day. Her sister readily agreed but spent a great deal of time chatting and catching up on family news and little time actually helping to produce cakes. Jill also asked her two older children to help her after school for a few hours each afternoon. Although not the best solution, it worked well for the first few weeks and then her children became involved in after-school activities and could no longer be counted on to be consistently available to help her in the kitchen. It was not until Jill had to make five cakes in one day and both children called to tell her they would not be home, that Jill decided she needed to seriously look for a stable workforce to help her make cakes.

As she explained her dilemma to her family they suggested she contact the Work Wagon, a nonprofit organization that found employment for adults who were homeless or in halfway houses by matching their abilities and skill levels to the employer's needs. Although it took a great deal of extra work on her part, Jill found the workers to be a relatively good, inexpensive labor force that was dedicated and willing to learn and work. She found that special care needed to be taken to ensure that workers were properly trained before operations would work smoothly and that often retraining was necessary. Jill also experienced the same concern with this group of workers that she had with her children; they often had health-related appointments or found other interests which kept them from consistently showing up when they were scheduled to work. In addition, many would often go back to their former living arrangements on the streets or would leave the city for other areas of the country.

Jill mulled over her current worker situation and product line schedule. With her one oven, she could bake two cakes at a time. She had performed a task and time assessment for the working day based on baking procedures, creating the boxes, and filling them with cakes and paper items. The task and time assessment found the estimated time for one complete package to be 2 hours and 55 minutes, with one hour at the end of each day devoted to specific decorating tasks and training.

Training was becoming a burden, and Jill was beginning to feel that all she did was train her workers, which was not why she had gotten into the cake business. She was not only doing the nightly ongoing training but she also had to train new employees. It took approximately three months of intense training before the new employees excelled at the tasks assigned to them. She was concerned about this since, in her mind, more time needed to be devoted to baking cakes and less time to training employees.

Promotional Activity

Although Jill had depended solely on word-of-mouth advertising to keep her business running, that was beginning to change. The Work Wagon featured her in the local newspaper as a smart, local businesswoman who hired many of their workers, teaching them a skill that would last them a lifetime. Through this simple publicity piece, Jill had seen her business almost double. She wondered what would happen if she began to advertise in that same local newspaper.

Thoughts of Expansion

As Jill was thinking over the leap to advertising in the local newspaper, her family was so enamored with her name in print and how much good her business was doing in the community that, over dinner one evening, they began to plant the seeds of expansion. Having taken a few accounting and marketing classes at the local community college a number of years before, Jill knew that to realistically think of selling cakes to people other than friends and family there were several things she would have to consider. She would have to review her cost and pricing situation, speak to the Work Wagon management or other sources about hiring more employees, and make numerous other decisions about the business. First, she would need to contact some contractors to discuss the costs of enlarging her kitchen. A preliminary but realistic estimate from her husband was $12,500 total. He had also learned that there were no zoning restrictions on expansion. Once she began to take expansion seriously, Jill realized she would need Debbie's help to establish a long-term strategic plan, particularly focusing on marketing.

Jill's Research

Before Jill could develop any strategic plan to increase her cake business she decided to gain additional information by talking to people in her hometown about their likes and dislikes when ordering gifts over the phone or through the mail. To accomplish this task and to keep her costs down, Jill asked eight close friends to come and had each of them bring five other people. A total of forty people came, which Jill broke into four different "focus groups"; an adequate number, she thought, to give her the required information.

Results from Jill's focus groups suggested several potential marketing opportunities in three key areas: (1) local customers who are looking for unique gift ideas, (2) businesses who would purchase cakes for incentives or gifts, and (3) customers outside her local area.

Jill needed to decide on many issues as she attempted to put together a plan. One set of issues pertained to marketing. She needed to decide what customer target segments she should aim at and the extent to which these should be local, regional, and/or national. She was unsure how she should reach potential customers with her message, as well as what that message should be, and whether anything should vary based on the target group. Because of the good publicity she had already received in the media, she thought that this might be an important future component of any promotion plans she assembled. Moreover, she was not clear about how customers would contact her. Things were simple enough if she stayed local; but going national might complicate this process considerably.

Timing of her promotion and production plans also hinges on dates for important holidays during future years, although she did not know which ones were most relevant. In addition, Jill was not sure that she could continue her single price for cakes. Her decision on cake prices could vary from a one-price approach to having a price differential for special-order customization outside of holiday orders. She was aware that many businesses used price incentives such as coupons or frequent-buyer plans, but she did not know whether this would be a viable approach for her business.

Jill estimated that during the first year of expanded operations she could sell an average of five cakes per day for the first three months, then increase by five orders per day quarterly, until she reached an average of twenty orders per day at the end of the first year. The second year, Jill hoped to double the first year's sales volume, and by the fifth year, she thought sales could reach fifty orders per day. Jill estimated that she would have to invest only $4,500 in advertising expenses to reach this sales level the first year, which she felt would drop to around the $1,000 range for succeeding years.

Jill estimated that she could produce cakes a total of 260 days each calendar year. She expected to pay wages of $5.25 per hour, for an eight-hour day to her workers, and a sales commission of 3 percent of sales. Administrative expenses were estimated at $1,500 per year. Her cost for shipping each cake is $3.00 unless a rush order is required, necessitating a 150 percent premium. Jill estimated the total production cost for 200 cakes as shown in Table C9.1 based on the supplies required. Table C9.2 shows the estimated production and assembly time for cakes.

Luncheon Meeting

Jill arrived at the restaurant before Debbie and, once again, wondered if she was doing the right thing by planning to expand her business. As she saw Debbie come through the front door with a big smile

TABLE C9.1. Total production costs for 200 cakes.

Business Supplies	Per 200 Cakes	Unit Size	Unit Cost
Baking supplies			
Pound cake mix	$42.72	50-lb. bag	$ 42.72
Glaze for lemon cake	35.57	50-lb. pail	35.57
Glaze for chocolate bunt	45.48	50-lb. pail	45.58
Chocolate chips	57.98	50-lb. box	57.98
Flavoring for lemon cake	15.00	12 oz.	15.00
Total	$196.75		
Packing supplies			
Tissue paper	$26.00	400 sheet/box	26.00
Shredded paper filler	21.00	10 lb.	21.00
Streamers/strings	3.51	3 oz.	3.51
Confetti	3.80	1-lb. box	3.80
Greeting card	200.00	100	100.00
Brochure	30.00	100	15.00
Hats	80.00	100	40.00
Horn	54.96	100	27.48
Balloon	12.50	144	9.00
Musical candle	400.00	36/box	72.00
Boxes	120.00	100	60.00
Silk screen	360.00	50	90.00
Total	$1,311.77		

TABLE C9.2. Cake production and assembly time.

Activity	Time
Production time per cake	
Preparation (start of each day)	15 minutes
Mixing	5 minutes
Pouring batter in pans	5 minutes
Baking	30 minutes
Cooling	30 minutes
Glazing	30 minutes
Drying of glaze	60 minutes
Wrapping	15 minutes
Cleanup (end of each day)	30 minutes
Assembly time per ten cakes	
Folding boxes	10 minutes
Folding paper	10 minutes
Placing items in box	10 minutes
Shrink wrap	20 minutes

on her face, she knew her response would be positive. As Debbie sat down, Jill pulled out her notes and was anxious for them to be incorporated into the business plan she needed. Debbie now had the task of producing a thorough and workable marketing strategy recommendation for Jill that included pro forma income statements for years one, two, and five.

Case 10

Sound Communications, Inc.

Robert Stevens
Philip Sherwood
David Loudon

Ray Mears has developed a portable sound system that he thinks will be able to offer him an additional income. As a music minister at a small local church, he has been searching for something to supplement his salary so that he can continue to afford to do what he loves (church music). With his knowledge of church and overseas missions audio system needs, he developed a sound system that is very versatile and affordable for such customers. He has established a company, Sound Communications, Inc., to begin to manufacture and market his design if it appears feasible.

Background

Having been in the ministry and overseas mission work for over twenty years, Mears recognized the need for a powerful yet portable sound system as a convenient way to communicate to small or large groups both indoors as well as outdoors under varying conditions. Many years ago, he had been given a small backpack system that had come from a Hollywood sound studio. It was very lightweight but not very powerful. He used it for several years until finally it was broken beyond repair. A member of one of Mears' overseas mission teams told him that it resembled a piece of PVC pipe and perhaps he should try to build one. This was the birth of the concept of the Power T.

This case is based on a student project by Brandon Dardeau, Dimitra Dourou, Claudia Inanex, and Sandy Hole, under the direct supervision of Robert Stevens.

Mears' Power T is a lightweight, portable sound system that can operate on AC/DC power and has a self-contained microphone, amplifier, and a speaker (see Figures C10.1 and C10.2, and Exhibit C10.1). The battery-powered system is completely portable and can even be used with a keyboard or other electrical musical instruments. The name of the product was originally going to be Port-a-Sound, in order to let the customer know that the unit provides sound in a portable unit.

Unfortunately, Mears had to change this name due to a possible trademark violation. He is not sure if the current name adequately reflects the features or benefits of the product to potential customers. Mears is confident of the attributes built into the product, but wonders if there are any other design features the product should have.

The product's exterior is a plastic (PVC pipe) outer shell that is a very durable protector of the inside of the unit. The two-way speaker system provides high-quality sound that is very effective for singing or for speaking in a normal-size room. In addition, if the customer needs to project to a large number of people either outside or in a very large room, the unit can accommodate additional speakers.

FIGURE C10.1. Components of the Power T.

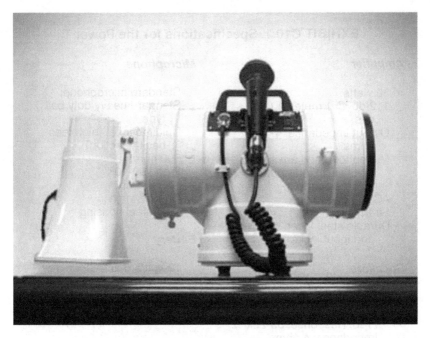

FIGURE C10.2. Assembled Power T.

The Power T also incorporates a horn speaker. The portable system has one audio input, so that the user can easily plug an auxiliary item directly into the unit (e.g., a cassette deck or a compact disc player). A microphone is attached to the unit, which provides high-quality and clear sound to the audience. The unit is totally self-contained and carries a one-year warranty against all factory defects.

Market Potential

Mears thinks the product has great potential—especially for schools, churches, and other organizations, particularly those that have outdoor events or the need for portable sound equipment (e.g., lifeguards at pools or on beaches). If the product has potential, Mears will be able to spend only a couple of days each week assembling and selling the Power T because he is a choir director at a church. This is his calling and his family needs the financial support provided by the position.

EXHIBIT C10.1. Specifications for the Power T.

Amplifier

30 watts
112 db @ 1 meter, 1,000
  cps
Output impedance: 4-16
  ohms
Microphone and auxiliary
  inputs with individual
  volume controls
AC/DC operation
Siren circuit
Durable steel faceplates
  and input jacks

Speakers

Main speaker:
  High quality 6.5" Two-way
  Freq. Response: 55-22kHz
  Impedance: 4 ohms
  Rated @ 60 watts continu-
  ous
  Metal protective grill
Horn:
  5" x 8" at face, heavy duty
  ABS plastic body with
  stainless steel hardware,
  rated @ 60 watts

Microphone

Standard microphone:
Standard heavy duty ball
  type
Unidirectional (high feed-
  back rejection)
600 ohms
Freq.: 90-10K
−75 +/−3db
On-off switch
Cast steel housing

Battery

12-volt/5.0 amp hours re-
  chargeable sealed lead
  acid
AC adapter/charger:
  12 VDC @ 1.5 amp

Weight

20 pounds (with standard
  accessories)

Dimensions

12" H x 21" W x 11" D

Mears has gathered some data and believes that the primary market for his product consists of two main groups. The first includes schools, colleges, and universities. The second market segment consists of organizations such as churches. A breakdown of the different types of potential purchasers in selected counties/parishes of three states is shown in Table C10.1. Even though there are other potential customers such as police departments, nursing homes, political groups, or even individuals or groups of singers, Mears' primary focus is on public and private schools, churches, and universities because of the perceived greater potential of these groups to purchase the product.

TABLE C10.1. Metropolitan statistical areas within 100 miles.

Counties/ Parishes*	Population	Schools	Churches	Univ./Colleges
South Arkansas				
Ashley	24,566	17	82	0
Bradley	11,587	7	39	0
Calhoun	5,727	3	20	0
Chicot	15,729	11	53	0
Clark	21,331	12	72	2
Cleveland	7,859	4	27	0
Columbia	25,733	16	86	1
Dallas	9,499	2	32	0
Desha	16,290	10	55	0
Drew	17,233	7	58	1
Hempstead	21,877	9	73	0
Lafayette	9,345	6	32	0
Lincoln	13,894	7	47	0
Nevada	9,938	5	34	0
Ouachita	29,541	15	99	0
Union	46,462	26	155	0
Total	286,611	157	964	4
West Mississippi				
Carroll	9,773	5	33	0
Claiborne	11,284	5	38	0
Copiah	28,288	7	95	0
Hinds	271,917	93	840	5
Holmes	21,036	14	71	0
Humpreys	11,717	7	40	0
Issaquena	1,732	0	6	0
Jefferson	8,500	11	29	0
Leflore	37,463	16	125	1
Madison	63,683	23	213	0
Rankin	96,280	30	321	0

TABLE C10.1 *(continued)*

Counties/ Parishes*	Population	Schools	Churches	Univ./Colleges
Sharkey	6,952	6	24	0
Sunflower	36,013	16	121	0
Warren	49,034	18	164	0
Washington	66,741	34	223	0
Yazoo	25,354	14	85	0
Total	745,767	299	2,428	6
North Louisiana				
Avoyelles	39,099	16	130	0
Bienville	15,750	8	53	0
Bossier	86,747	32	289	0
Caddo	246,325	93	822	2
Caldwell	9,787	14	33	0
Catahoula	11,101	10	37	0
Claiborne	17,234	12	58	0
Concordia	20,901	3	70	0
DeSoto	25,042	13	84	0
East Carroll	9,574	8	32	0
Franklin	22,168	14	74	0
Grant	17,596	8	59	0
Jackson	15,538	9	52	0
La Salle	13,714	9	46	0
Lincoln	42,490	19	144	2
Madison	12,156	7	41	0
Morehouse	31,892	16	107	0
Nachitoches	36,662	18	123	1
Ouachita	144,910	44	484	1
Rapides	130,554	62	435	1
Red River	9,256	6	31	0
Richland	20,340	14	68	0
Sabine	22,948	12	77	0

Counties/ Parishes*	Population	Schools	Churches	Univ./Colleges
Tensas	6,763	7	23	0
Union	20,814	10	70	0
Vernon	64,037	19	214	0
Webster	41,437	25	139	0
West Carroll	11,985	8	40	0
Winn	16,213	8	55	0
Total	1,163,033	524	3,890	7

*Louisiana only.

These organizations need compact and durable equipment that will withstand the wear and tear of everyday use. Pep rallies, choral events, and outdoor activities held by these groups usually presented the need for some type of sound equipment. The Power T is more flexible and powerful than the amplified megaphones used by many of these groups.

Mears' initial thinking about a marketing strategy has focused on a selling strategy in which he would cover an area involving a one-way driving distance of 100 miles. He thought this would allow him to make sales calls and return home the same day with relative ease. With such an approach, Mears thought he would be able to easily maintain his church music director job with no sacrifice in performance. Within the 100-mile radius, Mears determined that there were 980 schools, 7,282 churches, and 8 universities in a tri-state area including Arkansas, Louisiana, and Mississippi. He did not yet know the addresses of the specific organizations.

Competitive Analysis

After identifying what Mears thought were the most obvious target customers, he next tried to gain a better understanding of the competition. Mears thought that the Power T's main competitors would be amplified megaphones and portable sound systems since these are the most widely used systems in schools and churches. Even though these are the primary competitors, karaoke sound systems are also a threat due to the nature of the product (acceptable- to high-quality sound combined with one or more microphones for the purpose of singing). Currently, megaphones are the most commonly used communication tool in these target markets due to low cost and ease of use. However, Mears considered the Power T to have key advantages over its competitors due to certain attributes. Even though megaphones are portable, they do not provide a high-quality sound (especially for music) compared to the Mears Power T. Portable sound systems are also widely used by schools and churches. But Mears' product has a competitive advantage over this type of system because of its high mobility and AC/DC power flexibility. With its small size, just one person can carry, set up, and use it very easily. Component sound systems require AC power and generally require extra accessories, such as long cords and speakers, to be able to communicate with the audience.

The threat of future competition always exists due to the ease of entry into this type of market. The possibility of a competitor copying the product is a threat to be considered in this situation. Mears' Power T competition and approximate prices are shown in the following list.

Amplified Megaphone	$89.95
Karaokes	
Pioneer CLD-V880	$799.98
Pioneer CLD-V870	$699.98
Pioneer PD-V10G	$387.98
Pioneer PD-V10G (B)	$299.99
Zenesis K2-77	$169.00
Portable Sound Systems	
Fender Passport P-150	$424.99
Fender Passport PD-250	$849.99

Production

Ray Mears thinks it may be best for him to be solely responsible for all the marketing and production activities. He wants to manufacture the Power T by himself without outside labor. Mears has built several prototypes for trial and feedback from users. In the process, he has refined the operation down to an efficient activity. Production basically involves assembly of the component parts into a carrying case. The case contains all the components and also includes a handle with a clip for a microphone. The cost of the components is $210. By buying components in bulk he would be able to decrease variable costs by 10 percent and have the ability to build twenty units at a time. He can assemble one unit in an hour. With his current planned schedule of work, Mears anticipates that he will be able to assemble up to fifty units per month for sale and distribution. At this time he can only devote ten to twelve hours a week to production and sales of the product and still have time for his other responsibilities. Mears' hope is to produce enough revenue to provide an additional income of $35,000 per year.

Mears has lined up a finance company loan of $12,000 at 16 percent interest to move a small storage building onto his property to be used for manufacturing and storage. He will also use the loan to buy one month's supply of components. He felt he could interest potential investors in the product or acquire an additional loan if he could build and sustain a reasonable sales volume for six to twelve months.

Marketing

Mears would make personal sales calls on schools and churches to demonstrate the system and finalize sales. However, he is not at all sure that this is the most effective or profitable approach he could take. But he is confident that his knowledge of the product and the market's needs combined with his natural skills at communication would yield very good results through personal selling.

Mears has not yet finalized the other parts of his marketing strategy. He needs a prototype of a brochure that could be used in promotion to show to customers and leave behind where necessary. He does not know what other, if any, approaches he might need to take with promotion, their cost, or how he would go about planning and implementing any other alternative approaches.

Although being a one-man distribution approach for his product would allow him to control all aspects of the sale of the Power T, Mears does not know if that is how he should best spend his time and effort. In fact, he does not know what other options he might have for distribution of this product.

Mears plans to pay for all shipping costs in the delivery process if the unit must be shipped. If the customer is within a reasonable distance, then Mears plans to deliver the unit himself. He will be in charge of all phases of the distribution process. He will take, process, and fill all orders. If a unit is found to be defective within the warranty period of one year, then Mears must make the service call and repair the unit.

Another issue for Mears is what to charge for the Power T. The enthusiastic response he has received from friends in the music ministry encourages him to charge a premium price. But he feels ethically bound not to "gouge" the prospects he will be selling to. He has a reasonable grasp on the cost structure that will form the minimum price floor from which to work. A friend in the local school system has told him that an interesting policy in Louisiana bid law requires only those items costing $500 or more to be put out to bid. Mears assumes this must be representative of his other target states.

Market Opportunity Analysis Plan

A banker friend has told Mears that he could probably qualify for a traditional bank loan at 10 percent interest if he were to put together a thorough plan analyzing the business opportunity. He has decided this needs to be his next step in the process of getting the Power T to market and obtaining the supplemental income he desires.

Even more optimistically, if the Power T exceeded his present production and sales capacity levels within the next couple of years, it would present a challenge. Mears needs to have some contingency plans for a five-year period indicating how he would be able to take advantage of sales opportunities lying beyond the 100-mile range and production demands that could outstrip his present capabilities.

Appendix A

Secondary Data Sources
for Assessing Market Opportunities

A problem that confronts researchers in initiating a secondary data search is the massive amount, wide variety, and many locations of secondary data. Some method of logically summarizing the sources of secondary data is helpful. Most textbooks on the subject divide secondary data sources into two groups: internal and external data sources. Although Internet addresses are provided for many of the sources cited, the reader should be aware that the Web is ever-changing. Thus, some sites listed may no longer be accurate.

Internal secondary data sources are closest at hand since they are found within the organization initiating the research process. These internal data have been collected for other purposes but are available to be consolidated, compared, and analyzed to answer the new research question being posed. This is particularly true of organizations that have sophisticated management information systems that routinely gather and consolidate useful marketing, accounting, and production information.

Specific internal records or sources of internal secondary data are:

1. Invoice records
2. Income statements (various cost information)
3. Sales results
4. Advertising expenditures
5. Accounts receivable logs
6. Inventory records
7. Production reports and schedules
8. Complaint letters and other customer correspondence
9. Salesperson's reports (observations)
10. Management reports

This appendix was written by Bruce Wrenn. It has been adapted with the assistance of Kimberly Fellows from Bruce Wrenn, Robert Stevens, and David Loudon (2002). *Marketing Research: Text and Cases.* Binghamton, NY: The Haworth Press, pp. 65-78.

11. Service records
12. Accounts payable logs
13. Budgets
14. Distributor reports and feedback
15. Cash register receipts
16. Warranty cards

Even though most research projects require more than just internal data, this is a very cost-efficient place to begin the data search. Quite often a review of all internal secondary data sources will inexpensively give direction for the next phase of data collection. The internal search will give clues to what external data sources are required to gather the information needed to answer the research question.

External secondary data originate outside the confines of the organization. An overwhelming number of external sources of data are available to researchers. Good external secondary data may be found through libraries, Web searches, associations, and general guides to secondary data. Most trade associations accumulate and distribute information pertinent to their industry. Quite often this includes sales and other information gathered from their members. The *Directory of Directories* and the *Encyclopedia of Associations* are excellent sources for finding associations and organizations that may provide secondary information for a particular industry.

Data mining is the process by which companies extract consumer behavioral patterns from analysis of huge databases containing internally and externally generated data. These databases contain information gleaned from customer Web-site visits, warranty cards, calls to toll-free numbers, retail purchases, credit card usage, car registration information, home mortgage information, and thousands of other databases including the U.S. Census. The use of neural network and parallel processing technology allows marketers to search through these databases to find behavioral patterns which can help identify the best prospects for:

- Upgrading customers to more profitable products
- Cross-selling different products or services offered by the company
- Special offers or offers combining several companies (e.g., travel packages)
- Continued long-term relationship building
- "Weblining"—similar to the practice of "redlining," where vigorous customer service is reserved for only a firm's best customers and withheld from the marginal customers, all based on the customer records in the database[1]

The use of the Internet as a key channel of distribution has allowed many companies to develop even more sophisticated databases for marketing purposes.[2] For example, customers clicking on NextCard, Inc.'s ad for a credit card on the Quicken.com financial Web site can have their credit history checked and a card issue (or application rejected) in thirty-five seconds.

Secondary Data Sources on the World Wide Web

The Web has become the first, and too often the only, source to be used by the marketing researcher in search of pertinent secondary data. Most readers of this text have had experience "surfing the Web," and therefore are familiar with Web browsers (e.g., Netscape Navigator or Microsoft Internet Explorer); search engines or portals (e.g., Altaista, Infoseek, HotBot, Google, Excite, Yahoo!, etc.); indexes of business and other periodical literature (e.g., EBSCOHOST); Web search strategies (e.g., use of parentheses, and, or, not, +, −, quotation marks, asterisk, etc.); and use of newsgroups (e.g., Internet sites where people can post queries or respond other people's queries or post comments. Over 250,000 newsgroups exist, each devoted to a specific topic). The savvy researcher can harness these and other resources and methods of using the Internet to discover relevant secondary data available over the World Wide Web. The following are some useful Web sites for marketing researchers.

Meta-Sites or Sources of Research Reports

D&B Sales and Marketing Solutions: Provides tools such as a quarterly newsletter, business data, online catalog, marketing analysis tools, and free seminars that can help a marketer or business become more effective. It also provides information about how other businesses have increased their own marketing effectiveness. *www.b2bsalesandmarketing.com*

Dialog.com: This Web site provides information about business, law, science, finance, or engineering. It can help a researcher find company profiles and histories, brand information, periodicals, case studies, and career opportunities. It allows access to over 7,500 periodicals and journals from around the world and lets you analyze market moves and strategies, identify investment opportunities, track competitors worldwide, monitor product activities globally and follow new technologies and innovations. *www .dialog.com*

ECNext Knowledge Center: This site provides newsletters, profiles of varied companies, demographics of countries, and trade journals. It allows access to free citations, unlimited searching, and a research assistant tool that will notify you of additions to databases. *www.imrmall.com*

Factiva: This site combines information from the *Wall Street Journal,* and Dow Jones and Reuters news sources. Research data can be accessed in several languages. It offers a large archive of news and business information not available on the free Web, allowing users to conduct in-depth research on companies and industries. *www.factiva.com*

LexisNexis: This Web site aids in the search for business, tax, legal, and public record information among other topics. Search topics categorically, and access information through a variety of formats including print, online or CD-ROM. *www.lexis-nexis.com*

Marketing Research Association (MRA): This Web site can assist in marketing and opinion research. The tools available are data collectors, training advice and information, and a discussion forum for marketers to share thoughts and problems and possibly collaborate on various projects. *www .mra-net.org*

MarketResearch.com: This Web site compiles business information from around the world and makes its research available through this site. It promotes strategic planning by providing relevant research tools and techniques. *www.marketresearch.com*

Profound.com: This Web site provides market research and industry reports, publications, economic forecasts and analyses, patent and trademark information, and reports from analysts. *www.profound.com*

Quirk's Marketing Research Review: This Web site provides links to an Article Archive which includes case histories, *Researcher Forum, Research Directories,* and *Research Resources. www.quirks.com*

USADATA: This Web site provides useful techniques such as mailing lists, list solutions, and direct mail portals that can help with direct marketing. *www.usadata.com*

Research Associations

American Marketing Association: This Web site provides research information, case studies, and links to many additional marketing resources or services. *www.marketingpower.com*

The Council for Marketing & Opinion Research (CMOR): This Web site provides links to research, governmental affairs, and respondent cooperation. *www.cmor.org*

Council of American Survey Research Organizations (CASRO): This Web site provides access information about education and events, research, a video theater, and an industry newsletter. *www.casro.org/*

e-Telmar: This Web site provides access to thousands of marketing databases that are regularly used by advertisers, broadcasters, and publishers worldwide. *www.etelmar.com*

Market Research Society: This United Kingdom Web site provides links for news and jobs, industry profiles, and demographic and census information. Training, networking, conferences, publications, and links to agencies with close ties to the MRS can be found at this site. A forum is available for researchers to exchange information and advice. *www.marketresearch.org.uk*

National Mail Order Association (NMOA): This Web site provides information for resellers, manufacturers, service providers, and home-based business/office entrepreneurs. Find new products, industry contacts, legal forms, a bookstore, and newsletters here. *www.nmoa.org*

The Professional Marketing Research Society (PMRS): This Web site provides market research information in English and French. The "Resources" section provides a discussion forum, bookstore, and editorial board. *www .pmrs-aprm.com*

Qualitative Research Consultants Association (QRCA): Access a directory of over 700 consultants, advisors, interviewers, and focus groups from this home page. Also find in-depth definitions of the purposes and uses of qualitative research. *www.qrca.org*

Directories of Market Research Firms

Bluebook: The Marketing Research Association publishes an online directory of marketing research organizations—the *Bluebook.* Search the facilities and services database for companies that focus on marketing and opinion research. *www.bluebook.org*

Greenbook: This publication provided by the New York American Marketing Association is a global directory of companies specializing in marketing research or focus group services. *www.greenbook.org*

Marketing Research Firms and Syndicated Services

AC Nielsen: From this Web site one can access analysis, research, and information about products and services. Several tools such as retail measurement, consumer panel, customized research, and other services assist clients with making decisive marketing plans and provide researchers with cutting-edge information. *www.acnielsen.com*

Arbitron, Inc.: This service provides data and research from advertisers, broadcasters, cable companies, and other media outlets around the world. Measures audiences and studies consumer retail and purchasing patterns. These reports, based on a representative sample in each market, provide information concerning radio listening habits. *www.arbitron.com*

BehaviorScan: This site focuses on the consumer goods industry worldwide, provides store tracking, point-of-sale purchase data, brand preference information, consumer attitude analysis, and international statistics from more than twenty countries in the North America, Europe, and Latin America. This service, provided by Information Resources, Inc. (IRI), uses supermarket scanners to measure the consumption behavior of a panel of consumers. *www.infores.com/*

Burke Incorporated: This Web site provides qualitative research, custom marketing research, loyalty management, consulting, integration services, and retention management tools. *www.burke.com*

Find/SVP: This Web site offers advice and consultation about a variety of industries and business issues. Access information on strategic opportunities, industries and markets, benchmarking, and marketing trends. *www.findsvp.com*

Harris Interactive: This Web site allows one to perform strategic market research for specific groups such as the affluent, "tweens," people with chronic illnesses, and also access information about *The Harris Poll®*. *www.harrisinteractive.com/*

Information Resources, Inc. (IRI): This Web site focuses on the consumer goods industry worldwide. Provides store tracking, point-of-sale purchase data, brand preference information, consumer attitude analysis, and international statistics from more than twenty countries in the North America, Europe, and Latin America. *www.infores.com/*

M/A/R/C Research: This Web site offers tools, techniques, and analysis for maximizing marketing potential. *www.marcresearch.com*

Maritz Marketing Research: This Web site provides information about performance improvement, travel, and marketing research information. Also find information on topics such as creating bonds between companies and audiences, driving sales staff performance, and valuing customer loyalty. *www.maritz.com*

National Purchase Diary Panel (NPD): This diary panel of several thousand households provides monthly purchase information about approximately fifty product categories. This site offers marketing and sales information, tracking services, specialty products, industry publications, and proprietary research. Information from the toy, apparel, and consumer electronics industries (among many others) can also be accessed. *www.npd.com*

Nielsen Media Research: Perhaps the most well-known service, the Nielsen Television Index measures television show ratings and shares among a panel of television viewers who are matched according to U.S. national statistics. Radio, television, advertising, and print periodical information from over seventy countries are available on this Web site. *www.nielsenmedia research.com*

RoperASW: This Web site provides up-to-date marketing information about such things as brand strategies, customer loyalty, corporate reputation, communications, consumer trends, demographics, market analyses, healthcare studies, product launching, and positioning. Available surveys deal with public opinion on social, political, and economic subjects. *www.roperasw.com/*

Simmons MRB Media/Marketing Service: This Web site tracks American consumer lifestyles, including purchases and preferences. Find details of a National Consumer Study (NCS), and cross-cultural surveys that include Spanish and English speakers. Based on extensive data collection from a national sample of about 20,000 individuals, this service reports information concerning media exposure as well as purchase behavior about several hundred product categories. Simmons offers a software package (Choices), which allows the user to create almost unlimited comparisons and cross-tabulations of the extensive database. *www.smrb.com/*

Starch Readership Reports: This site provides advertising, marketing, and opinion research. Find information about the Starch Report, which tracks the effectiveness of various forms of print advertising. These reports provide measures of exposure to print ads in a wide variety of magazines and newspapers using a large number of personal interviews. *www2.una.edu/ kabsher/StarchReadershipService.htm*

Synovate: This Web site provides census information and business data, segmentation systems, and other marketing tools. *www.synovate.com*

Consumer Data Sources

Census of the Population: Taken every ten years, this source reports the population by geographic region, with detailed breakdowns according to demographic characteristics, such as gender, marital status, age, education, race, income, etc. *www.gpoaccess.gov/index.html*

Consumer Market and Magazine Report: Published annually, this source describes the household population of the United States with respect to a number of demographic variables and consumption statistics. The profiles are based on a large probability sample and they give good consumer behavioral and socioeconomic characteristics. *www2.una.edu/kabsher/Starch ReadershipService.htm*

County and City Data Book: This Bureau of the Census publication gives statistics on population, income, education, employment, housing, retail, and wholesale sales for various cities, MSAs (metropolitan statistical areas), and counties. *www.census.gov/prod/www/ccdb.html*

Historical Statistics of the United States from Colonial Times to 1957: This volume was prepared as a supplement to the *Statistical Abstract*. This source provides data on social, economic, and political aspects of life in the United States. It contains consistent definitions and thus eliminates incompatibilities of data in the Statistical Abstracts caused by dynamic changes over time. *www.census.gov/statab/www/*

Marketing Information Guide: Published monthly by the Department of Commerce, this source lists recently published studies and statistics that serve as a useful source of current information to marketing researchers. *www.commerce.gov*

Rand McNally Commercial Atlas and Marketing: Published annually, this source contains marketing data and maps for some 100,000 cities and towns in the United States. It includes such things as population, auto registrations, basic trading areas, manufacturing, transportation, population, and related data. *www.randmcnally.com*

Sales & Marketing Management Survey of Buying Power: Published annually by *Sales & Marketing Management* magazine, this source provides information such as population, income, retail sales, etc., again broken down by state, county, and MSA, for the United States and Canada. *www.sales andmarketing.com*

Competitive Data Sources

Almanac of Business and Industrial Financial Ratios: Published annually by Prentice-Hall, this source lists a number of businesses, sales, and certain operating ratios for several industries. The computations are from tax returns, supplied by the IRS, and the data allow comparison of a company's financial ratios with competitors of similar size. *www.prenticehall.com*

Business Publication Rates and Data: Published by Standard Rate & Data Service, Inc., this index lists various trade publication sources. *www.srds .com*

Directory of Corporate Affiliations: Published annually by National Register Publishing Company, Inc., this source lists approximately 3,000 parent companies and their 16,000 divisions, subsidiaries, and affiliates. *www .nationalregisterpub.com/*

Directory of Intercorporate Ownership: Published by Simon & Schuster, Volume 1 contains parent companies, with divisions, subsidiaries, overseas subsidiaries, and American companies owned by foreign firms. Volume 2 provides an alphabetical listing of all the entries in Volume 1. *www .simonsays.com*

Fortune Directory: Published annually, this source presents information on sales, assets, profits, invested capital, and employees for the 500 largest U.S. industrial corporations. *www.fortune.com*

Fortune Double 500 Directory: Published annually in the May-August issues of *Fortune* magazine, this source offers information on assets, sales, and profits of 1,000 of the largest U.S. firms, fifty largest banks, life insurance companies, and retailing, transportation, utility, and financial companies. In addition, this source ranks foreign firms and banks. *www.fortune .com*

Middle Market and *Million Dollar Directories:* Published annually by Dun & Bradstreet, these sources list companies with assets in the range of $500,000 to $999,999 and $1 million+. The directories offers information on some 30,000 companies' officers, products, sales, and number of employees. *www.dnb.com/us*

Moody's Manuals: This source list includes manuals entitled *Banks and Finance, Municipals and Governments, Public Utilities, and Transportation,* which contain balance sheet and income statements for various companies and government units. The *Industrial Manual,* published annually, provides information on selected companies' products and description, history, mergers and acquisition record, principal plants and properties, principal offices, as well as seven years of financial statements and statistical records. The *Manual of Investments* documents historical and operational data on selected firms and five years of their balance sheets, income accounts, and dividend records. *www.moodys.com*

Reference Book of Corporate Managements: Published annually by Dun & Bradstreet, this source gives a list of 2,400 companies and their 30,000 officers and directors. *www.loc.gov/rr/business/duns/duns3.html*

Sheldon's Retail Directory of the United States and Canada: Published annually by Phelon, Sheldon & Marsar, Inc., this source supplies the largest chain, department, and specialty stores, by state and city, and by Canadian province and city. This source also includes merchandise managers and buyers.

Standard and Poor's Register of Corporations, Directors, and Executives: Published annually, this source provides officers, sales, products, and number of employees for some 30,000 U.S. and Canadian corporations. *www.netadvantage.standardandpoors.com*

State Manufacturing Directories: Published for each state, these directories give company addresses, products, officers, etc., by geographic location. *http://mnistore.com/*

Thomas Register of American Manufacturers: Published annually, this source gives specific manufacturers of individual products, as well as the company's address, branch offices, and subsidiaries. *www.thomasregister.com*

Wall Street Journal Index: Published monthly, this source lists corporate news, alphabetically, by firm name, as it has occurred in the *Wall Street Journal. www.wallstreetjournal.com*

Market Data Sources

American Statistics Index: A Comprehensive Guide and Index to the Statistical Publications of the U.S. Government: Published monthly by the Congressional Information Service, this source indexes statistical publications of federal agencies, and it is a useful starting point for obtaining market data. *www.lexisnexis.com/academic/3cis/cise/AmericanStatisticsIndex.asp*

Ayer Directory of Publications: Published annually by Ayer Press, this source is a comprehensive listing of newspapers, magazines, and trade publications of the United States, by state, Canada, Bermuda, Republics of Panama and the Philippines, and the Bahamas. *www.galegroup.com*

Bureau of the Census Catalog: Published quarterly, this source is a comprehensive guide to Census Bureau publications. Publications include agriculture, foreign trade, governments, population, and the economic census. *www.access.gpo.gov*

Business Conditions Digest: Published monthly by the Bureau of Economic Analysis, Department of Commerce, this source gives indications of business activity in table and chart form. *www.access.gpo.gov*

Business Cycle Developments: This monthly source from the Bureau of the Census provides some seventy business activity indicators that give keys to general economic conditions. *www.access.gpo.gov*

Business Statistics: Published biennially by the Department of Commerce, this source is a supplement to "The Survey of Current Business." It provides information from some 2,500 statistical series, starting in 1939. *www.doc.gov*

Census of Business: Published every five years, this source supplies statistics on the retail, wholesale, and service trades. The census of service trade compiles information on receipts, legal form of organization, employment, and number of units by geographic area. *www.access.gpo.gov*

Census of Manufacturers: Published every five years, this source presents manufacturers by type of industry. It contains detailed industry and geographic statistics, such as the number of establishments, quantity of output, value added in manufacture, employment, wages, inventories, sales by customer class, and fuel, water, and energy consumption. *www.access.gpo. gov*

Census of Retail Trade: Taken every five years, in years ending in 2 and 7, this source provides information on 100 retail classifications arranged by SIC numbers. Statistics are compiled on number of establishments, total sales, sales by product line, size of firms, employment and payroll for states, MSAs, counties, and cities of 2,500 or more. *http://bookstore .gpo.gov/*

Census of Selected Service Industries: Taken every five years, in years ending in 2 and 7, this source compiles statistics on 150 or more service classifications. Information on the number of establishments, receipts, payrolls, etc., is provided for various service organizations. *http://bookstore.gpo .gov/*

Census of Transportation: Taken every five years, in years ending in 2 and 7, this source presents three specific surveys: Truck Inventory and Use Survey, National Travel Survey, and Commodity Transportation Survey. *http: //bookstore.gpo.gov/*

Census of Wholesale Trade: Taken every five years, in years ending in 2 and 7, this source provides statistics of 118 wholesale classifications. Information includes numbers of establishments, sales, personnel, payroll, etc. *http://bookstore.gpo.gov/*

Commodity Yearbook: Published annually by the Commodity Research Bureau, this source supplies data on prices, production, exports, stocks, etc., for 100 commodities. *www.crbtrader.com*

County Business Patterns: Published annually, this source from the Departments of Commerce and Health, Education, and Welfare gives statistics on the number of businesses by type and their employment and payroll broken down by county. *www.hhs.gov*

Directories of Federal Statistics for Local Areas and for *States: Guides to Sources:* These two directories from the Bureau of the Census list sources of federal statistics for local areas, and for states, respectively. Data includes such topics as population, health, education, income, finance, etc. *www.census.gov*

Directory of Federal Statistics for Local Areas: A Guide to Sources: This source looks at topics such as population, finance, income, education, etc., in a local perspective. *www.access.gpo.gov*

Economic Almanac: Published every two years by The Conference Board, this source gives data on population, prices, communications, transportation, electric and gas consumption, construction, and mining and manufacturing output, in the United States, Canada, and other selected world areas. *www.conference-board.org*

Economic Census: This publication is a comprehensive canvass of U.S. industrial and business activities, taken by the Census Bureau every five years. In addition to providing the framework for forecasting and planning, these censuses provide weights and benchmarks for indexes of industrial production, productivity, and price. Management uses these in economic or sales forecasting, and analyzing sales performance, allocating advertising budgets, locating plants, warehouses and stores, and so on. *www.gpoaccess .gov/index.html*

Economic Indicators: Published monthly by the Council of Economic Advisors, Department of Commerce, this source gives current, key indicators of general business conditions, such as GNP (gross national product), personal consumption expenditures, etc. *www.access.gpo.gov*

Encyclopedia of Associations: Published by Gale Research Co., this will acquaint a researcher with various associations for cost data pertaining to a desired industry. *www.gale.com*

Federal Reserve Bulletin: Published monthly, this publication offers financial data on interest rates, credit, savings, banking activity; an index of industrial production; and finance and international trade statistics. *www .federalreserve.gov/pubs/bulletin/default.htm*

Market Guide: This annual source presents data on population, principal industries, transportation facilities, households, banks, and retail outlets for some 1,500 U.S. and Canadian newspaper markets. *www.editorand publisher.com*

Measuring Markets: A Guide to the Use of Federal and State Statistical Data: This publication lists federal and state publications covering population, income, employment, taxes. and sales. It is a useful starting point for the marketing researcher who is interested in locating secondary data. *www.access.gpo.gov*

Merchandising: Information regarding the "Statistical and Marketing Report" and the "Statistical and Marketing Forecast" can be accessed from this Web site. The first report provides such information as sales, product saturation, and import/export data. The latter can assist in forecasting market factors, and provides manufacturers' sales estimates for the upcoming year. *www.theparagongroup.com/presentations/MarketDataSources.pdf*

Monthly Labor Review: Published monthly by the U.S. Bureau of Labor Statistics, this source compiles trends and information on employment, wages, weekly working hours, collective agreements, industrial accidents, etc. *www.bls.gov/opub/mlr/mlrhome.htm*

Predicasts: This company provides research on companies, products, technologies and markets from business and financial publications, trade journals and newspapers, market research studies, industry newsletters, news releases, and investment and brokerage firm reports. *www.virtualref.com/ _verifier/275.htm*

Standard and Poor's Industry Survey: Published annually, this source offers current surveys of industries and a monthly Trends and Projections section, useful in forecasting market factors. *www.netadvantage.standardand poors.com*

Standard and Poor's Trade and Securities Statistics: Published monthly, this source contains statistics on banking, production, labor, commodity prices, income, trade, securities, etc. *www.standardandpoors.com*

Standard Corporation Records: Published by Standard and Poor Corporation (NY), this is a publication of financial reporting data of the larger firms. *www.netadvantage.standardandpoors.com*

Statistical Abstract of the United States: Published annually by the Bureau of the Census, this source serves as a good initial reference for other secondary data sources. It includes data tables covering social, economic, industrial, political, and demographic subjects. *www.access.gpo.gov.*

Statistics of Income: Published annually by the Internal Revenue Service, this source gives balance sheet and income statement statistics, prepared from federal income tax returns of corporations, and broken down by major industry, asset size, etc. *www.irs.gov/taxstats/index.html*

Survey of Current Business: Published monthly by the Bureau of Economic Analysis, Department of Commerce, this source presents indicators of general business, personal consumption expenditures, industry statistics, domestic trade, earnings and employment by industry, real estate activity, etc. *www.access.gpo.gov*

U.S. Industrial Outlook: Published annually, this source provides a detailed analysis of approximately 200 manufacturing and non-manufacturing industries. It contains information on recent developments, current trends, and a ten-year outlook for the industries. This source is useful in forecasting the specific marketing factors of a market analysis. *http://bookstore.gpo .gov/*

Indexes of Periodicals

Business Periodicals Index: This source lists articles by subject heading from 150 or more business periodicals. It also suggests alternate key words that can be used to determine a standard of relevance in environmental analysis. *www.hwwilson.com/newdds/wp.htm*

Ebsco Information Services: Ebsco provides information management through electronic journals, database management, and access to online databases and publications. *www.ebsco.com*

Public Affairs Information Services Bulletin (PAIS): Similar to, but different from, the Business Periodicals Index, this source includes more foreign publications, and it includes many books, government publications, and many nonperiodical publications. *www.pais.org/index.stm*

Reader's Guide to Periodical Literature: This index presents articles from magazines of a general nature, such as *U.S. News and World Report, Time, Newsweek, Saturday Review,* etc. It also suggests alternate key words that provide initial insight into the nature of the environment. *www.virtualref .com/_verifier/98.htm*

Appendix B

Sample Market Opportunity Analysis Report

OPPORTUNITY ANALYSIS
FOR ROLLCO PACKAGING COMPANY

Executive Summary

Four major considerations in assessing the economic feasibility of the proposed Rollco Packing Company are:*

1. Is there sufficient demand for beef and pork products in the three-state market area to justify the establishment of an additional slaughtering operation?

An analysis of the population and consumption patterns for the three-state area compared to total output of present slaughtering operations in this three-state area shows a net excess of consumption when stated in animal equivalents of 1,846,700 cattle and 2,373,700 hogs. Projections of future demand indicate a further increase in the consumption of both beef and pork products for the market area. Therefore, it is concluded that there would be ample demand for the output of the proposed facility operating at the level of production of 93,750 hogs and 93,750 cattle annually.

2. Is there sufficient supply of animals in the area of the proposed facility to support the proposed level of output of 93,750 cattle and 93,750 hogs annually?

Although there is a large inventory of cattle and hogs in the three-state area, the number of cattle available for slaughter is considerably lower than the inventory would indicate. The absence of feedlot operations in the area would necessitate the importation of approximately 20 percent of the cattle output of the facility. This would be approximately 18,750 cattle of the higher grades. With the present marketing of animals within the area and the proposed sales facility at Columbus, USA, it is probable that the 75,000

---

* Data provided in this report have been disguised.

cattle of lower grades could be acquired within the immediate area. Enough hogs to support the proposed level of operation of the plant are available in the market area.

3. *Can the proposed facility operate at a profit with the current market prices for beef and pork carcasses, proposed level of output, and the investment necessary to establish the proposed facility?*

Annual revenues from the sale of carcasses and offal would total $46,997,888. Annual expenses for this level of production would total $45,038,237. The proposed facility could therefore operate at an annual net profit of $1,028,817 after taxes. These figures reflect average 2005 prices for animal inputs and carcasses.

4. *Will the profit realized from the operation of the proposed facility justify the investment?*

The rate of return (investment divided by net profit) on the capital requirements of the $5,784,282 for the proposed operation would be only 17.77 percent. Using the excess PV technique to compare the PV of the returns (net profit plus depreciation) that can be expected over the life of the proposed facility with the capital requirements for establishing the proposed venture, it is concluded that the proposed venture is economically feasible. The annual cash flows produce a return in excess of 15 percent.

Introduction

Purpose

The purpose of this study was to determine the economic feasibility of a "kill and chill" operation to be located in Columbus, USA. The study focused on the monetary feasibility of such an operation. This involved a preliminary assessment of markets for outputs and inputs of the proposed operation, projections of revenues and operating costs, and analysis of the anticipated ROI.

Preliminary Assumptions

Several basic assumptions were made in developing the substantive materials which were analyzed in reaching the conclusions seated in the last section of the report.

Because of the anticipated size of the operation, it was assumed that the plant would be federally inspected so that sales could be made in interstate commerce. Inspection is performed by the Meat Inspection Division of the Agricultural Research Service of the USDA. All meat which moves in interstate commerce must be federally inspected.

Second, it was assumed that the proposed plant would concentrate on the market area represented by the three states. The market potential existing in these states and the anticipated size of the operation warrant such an assumption as will be shown in the report.

The third assumption dealt with the exact nature of the operation. It was assumed that the plant would not be an integrated operation. That is, no feedlot operations would be maintained (other than that necessary to service working inventory) and no additional processing of slaughtered animals would take place. This assumption is based on information provided by the originators of the project and is vital in determining both costs and revenues to be derived from the proposed operation.

A final assumption was that the plant would operate at a predetermined level and sell its entire output. Certain basic facilities are required to start such an operation. However, the utilization of such equipment may vary considerably due to seasonal variations in the availability of cattle and hogs and changes in the market for the products of the firm. This specified level of operation would entail slaughtering an average of 375 cattle and 375 hogs daily. Using a 250 workday calendar, this would result in an annual slaughter of 93,750 cattle and 93,750 hogs or a 187,500 annual slaughter. (The average output of such plants is 22,500 heads annually.) This production and sales level is vital to the analysis to follow. Operating at same other level of output than the one specified would substantially influence cost and revenues and would not be reflected in the analysis presented in this report.

It should also be pointed out that no attempt was made to analyze the managerial abilities of administrative personnel of the proposed plant. This was beyond the scope of this particular study. However, the profitability of any business operation is dependent on the possession of adequate managerial abilities by those personnel responsible for the decision making within the organization.

Other assumptions are noted in the report where they are needed to facilitate the analysis.

Market Potential for Beef and Pork

Consumer Demand

Per capita consumption of beef in the United States is an all-time high—116 pounds. This figure represents an increase of six pounds per capita in the ten-year period from 1995 to 2005. Consumption may reach 150 pounds per capita by 2009.

The consumption of pork has also been increasing. Comparable figures are 63 pounds per capita in 1995, 67 pounds in 2005, and an anticipated 70 pounds per capita in 2009.

Tables B.1 and B.2 combine population figures for the market area—the three market area states—with per capita consumption values to yield total consumption of beef and pork respectively. These values are then converted into the equivalent number of beef cows and hogs required to meet the consumption levels. These tables therefore show the number of beef cows and hogs consumed in the market area in 2005.

Market potential is defined as the maximum capacity of a market to purchase a specific type of offering in a specified time period. As shown in these two tables, consumption in the three-state area represents considerable market potential. The equivalent of over two million beef cows and four million hogs were consumed in this three-state area in 2005. These calculations are based on 2005 population and consumption estimates, and it should be noted that this is a conservative estimate of potential for the proposed plant. By the time the plant would begin operations, there would have been an increase in both population and average consumption of beef and pork.

TABLE B.1. Estimated market area beef cow consumption for 2005.

State	Population	Per Capita Beef Consumption (Pounds)	Total Beef Consumption (1,000 head)	Beef Cow Equivalents
State 1	4,402,000	116	510,630,000	945.6
State 2	4,667,000	116	541,370,000	1,002.5
State 3	2,836,875	116	329,080,000	609.4
	11,905,875		1,381,080,000	2,557.5

TABLE B.2. Estimated market area pork consumption for 2005.

State	Population	Per Capita Pork Consumption (Pounds)	Consumption (Pounds)	Total Pork/Hog Equivalent (1,000 head)
State 1	4,402.000	67	294,930,000	2,021.0
State 2	4,667,000	67	312,690,000	2,141.8
State 3	2,836,875	67	190,070,000	1,301.9
	11,905,875		797,690,000	5,464.7

Availability of Livestock Supplies

The proposed plant will be unable to secure adequate supplies of livestock from within the market area. In fact, a recent publication of the Research and Development Center in Columbus states that about 50 percent of all animals slaughtered in State 3 came from other states. The following list shows the inventory of cattle and hogs in the market area in 2005.

State	Cattle	Hogs
State 1	2,563	1,374
State 2	2,384	369
State 3	3,266	750
Total	8,213	2,493

Although the marketing of cattle and calves exceed slaughter in the market area, most of those marketed are calves that are shipped to large feedlots in the West. The relatively large inventory of cattle and hogs is thus somewhat misleading. Since it is more economical to ship calves out West and feed them than to ship feed into the market area, the number of cattle available for slaughter is substantially less than the inventory would indicate. The same situation is generally true of hogs. This lack of slaughter animals in the market area can be shown more clearly in Table B.3. This table shows

TABLE B.3. Consumption, slaughter, and imports of beef and pork in states 1, 2, and 3, 2005 (1,000 head).

State	Consumption[a]	Slaughter[b]	Imports
Beef			
State 1	945.6	125.5	820.1
State 2	1,002.5	233.4	769.1
State 3	609.4	351.9	257.5
Total	2,557.5	710.8	1,846.7
Pork			
State1	2,021.0	1,194.4	826.6
State 2	2,141.8	290.3	1,851.5
State 3	1,301.9	1,606.3	−304.4[c]
Total	5,464.7	3,091.0	2,373.7

[a]1,000 head equivalents.
[b]Slaughter figures based on 2005 farm slaughter values.
[c]Slaughter of pork exceeded consumption in State 3.

consumption and slaughter of cattle and hogs in the three-state area and the imports of animals needed to meet consumption levels.

The equivalent of 1,846,700 beef cows and 2,373,700 hogs had to be imported into the three-state area to satisfy consumption needs in 2005.

Thus far, two basic facts have been established: (1) the excess of consumption over slaughter in the market area establishes the existence of adequate potential for another slaughtering operation in the areas, and (2) the large amount of beef imported into the area to satisfy market demands indicates that only a portion of the slaughter animals for the proposed plant could be supplied from within the area. The additional supplies (higher grades of animals) would have to be purchased outside the market area and shipped in at higher prices.

The excess of hog slaughter over consumption in the state indicates that supplies of hogs in the area would probably be sufficient to support the anticipated levels of production.

Market Prices—Animal Inputs

One of the major factors determining the profitability of the proposed operation is the cost of raw materials—cattle and hogs. For purposes of analysis, it was assumed that 20 percent of the cattle slaughtered by the plant would come from outside the market area. This assumption is based on the results of the analysis of the availability of animals previously discussed. At the proposed slaughter level of 93,750 cattle annually, this would mean that 18,750 slaughter animals would have to be procured from outside the market area and 75,000 from within the area. All of the hogs slaughtered would be supplied from within the local area.

Even though the market for cattle and hogs was in such a state of uncertainty during the time period of the study, it was felt that a reasonable approach to determining prices of inputs and outputs was taken. Although these prices may change substantially by the time the actual operations begin, the margin of difference between the sets of prices should remain fairly constant.

The average price per hundredweight of beef cattle and hogs was $43.15 and $31.40 respectively for the United States in 2005. The average price for cattle and hogs in State 3 was $40.55 and $32.00 for the same period.

In this study, the prices of $43.15 per hundredweight for beef cows from outside the area and $40.55 for those obtained within the area were used in computations. The hog price of $32.00 per hundredweight was used as the relevant hog input price. The difference in prices for beef inputs seems reasonable since the beef obtained outside the area would be higher-grade animals.

Transportation costs for animals obtained from outside the market area would also be different. Interviews with local truck operators and packing companies indicate that the rates for transportation of livestock is in a state of change toward higher rates and a difference in methods used in computing rate. Both will cause higher transportation costs in the future.

In computing transportation cost, a rate of 75¢ per hundredweight was used for animals acquired within the market area and $1.13 per hundredweight for animals brought in from outside the market area.

Cost of the Facility

Land Costs

The proposed slaughtering facility is to be located ten miles south of Columbus, USA, on State 3 Highway 7; fifty-four miles southeast of Baytown; thirty-four miles north of Saytown; 124 miles from New Cravens; and forty-three miles from Tunis. This location places the proposed facility in an area which is relatively central to the major population concentration in the market area. This area also seems to have an adequate labor supply, is a major livestock producing area, and has relatively low land values for industrial development of $2,439 per acre. Although this figure is somewhat higher than average land prices of $935 to $1,250 per acre for similar land around Columbus, it is considerably lower than comparable land nearer major population areas and the appraised value of the land.

One hundred acres have been acquired by the corporation in exchange for stock. The total cost for this land is $243,900. Immediate space requirements for the plant facility, holding pens sufficient for at least 750 cattle and 750 hogs, parking lots and truck loading docks, water well sites, adequate expansion space, and sewage treatment facilities would not exceed fifteen acres.

One hundred acres is thus far in excess of the actual space requirement needs and the expenditure for this amount substantially influences the rate of ROI.

Conversely, there are several possible arguments in favor of initial acquisition of the total acreage. First, it provides the company with control of the environment in which the plant is located. This would enable the company to undertake future expansion into auxiliary processing operations or vertical integration of a feeding operation should economic conditions warrant. Second, once the proposed plant is in operation, land adjacent to it would increase in value above the present costs. And finally, any additional industrial development could be controlled by the company and would be an important fact in encouraging related industry, as well as becoming an additional source of revenue for the company. No attempt was made to judge the relative merits of these arguments.

Building Costs

Table B.4 shows the breakdown of building costs for the proposed facility. These cost estimates were provided by Martin Supplies, Inc., Kansas City, Kansas. Although architectural specifications would be necessary for an accurate estimate of building costs, these estimates at an average of $40.50 per square foot seem to be somewhat high. Local estimates supplied by the originators of the project were approximately $25 per square foot. The local estimate includes the special building characteristics required of a federally inspected slaughter facility. This is an average figure for the total building, with the processing areas higher and nonprocessing areas at a much lower rate. Using local estimates, the cost of the plant facility would be $793,850.

The accuracy of the estimate of building costs will substantially influence the capital required to initiate the project. A variance of $51 per square

TABLE B.4. Breakdown of building costs estimates—Rollco Packaging Company.

	Measurements	Sq. Ft.	Cost per Sq. Ft.	Total Cost
Basement	72 × 126	9,072	$37.50	$340,200
Kill floor	72 × 126	9,072	43.75	396,900
Beef chill	40 × 64	2,560	43.75	112,000
Beef cooler	42 × 64	2,688	43.75	117,600
Hog cooler	32 × 50	1,600	43.75	70,000
Edible cooler	13 × 50	650	43.75	28,440
Cutting room	48 × 48	2,304	40.00	92,160
Dry storage	12 × 40	480	37.50	18,000
Shipping dock	64 × 12	768	40.00	30,720
Office	80 × 32	2,560	31.25	80,000
Total		31,754	40.50	$1,286,020
Individual Costs				
Building cost				$1,286,020.00
Equipment cost				1,036,821.00
Site preparation				31,250.00
Sewer system				62,500.00
Engineering				62,500.00
Road work				37,500.00
Preliminary total estimate of project				$2,516,591.00

foot would amount to a $40,500 error. Therefore, without architectural plans and a firm bid from a local contractor, it must be assumed that the estimate provided by Martin Supplies is the best present estimate available since it reflects the judgment of a firm experienced in the construction of slaughtering facilities. The present figures include allowances for parking and holding pens sufficient for 750 cattle and 750 hogs, which is a two-day supply at the state level of output. According to federal regulations, holding pens must be paved with curbs. Parking areas must also be hard-surface to keep airborne particles to an acceptable level. Local estimates do not include these features. Also, according to information supplied by the originators of the project, the Martin estimates include an additional 15 percent to offset possible increases in building materials and labor costs before the facility could be built. This would account for $193,131 of the discrepancy between the two estimates. The remaining $300,568 difference in estimates is an amount in excess of the possible costs of holding pens and parking facilities. It may be a reflection of the differences in labor costs for construction between Kansas City and Columbus. Verifying the accuracy of these estimates is beyond the scope of the present investigation and perhaps not possible without architectural plans which are not available. Therefore, the Martin estimates will be used in the financial and economic analysis as the best present estimate of the complete facility including building, holding pens, parking and loading facilities.

The following list shows other building costs estimates supplied by Martin Supplies, Inc. Since the land required does not have existing water and sewage treatment facilities adequate to handle the needs of the proposed slaughtering facility, these costs are shown here. Again, these figures are 15 percent above present costs to offset effects of inflation before actual construction can be completed. This is $29,065 in excess of present costs.

Site preparation	$31,250
Sewer system	62,500
Engineering	62,500
Road work	37,500
Total	$193,750

Federal regulations and practical considerations require that access roads in the vicinity of the plant be hard-surface. Costs for drilling two 900 foot water wells and construction of a tank to meet the needs of the proposed facility of 30,000 gallons per hour are not included due to lack of available data.

Equipment Costs

An itemized listing and current prices of equipment necessary to outfit the proposed facility is included in Appendix 8 (not shown here). Total equipment costs for Martin Supplies, Inc., Kansas City, Kansas, are $1,036,821. The equipment listed and the prices quoted are in competition with industry rates and that the equipment is adequate for the type of operation and the proposed level of output of the facility. Transportation of equipment to the plant site and installation are not included in these figures. Average industry transportation costs are five percent of sales price and installation costs are 17 percent of sales price. Again, the equipment prices are 15 percent above current prices to offset future price increases before the plant can be completed. For the purposes of this report, the 15 percent will be used to partially offset transportation and installation charges. Should price increases occur before the plant is constructed, it is possible that total costs for equipment, installation, and transportation to the plant site would be considerably higher than the total shown here.

All fixed cost estimates supplied by Martin Supplies, Inc., are 15 percent above current costs. This is a total of $222,195.

In addition, the difference between costs estimates of the building from Martin and local contractors is $443,699. This would provide $665,895 to cover construction of holding pens, water supply, transportation, and installation of equipment, architectural fees, and parking areas. Assuming a certain amount of inaccuracy in the estimates of local contractors without firm bids or architectural specifications, it is probable that the costs estimates by Martin are sufficiently inflated to cover the nonspecific items mentioned and retain a comfortable cushion for possible future price increases. The breakdown of costs estimates supplied by Martin is considered to be quite unrealistic in any instances, but the overall cost estimate of the facility and equipment is the highest possible cost, assuming that the facility could be built for considerably less than these estimates. This would substantially reduce the capital investment and also affect estimates of the rate of return of investment. The following list summarizes the total costs of the facility.

Source	Cost
Land	$243,875
Building	1,287,549
Other building costs	193,750
Equipment	1,036,321
Total	$2,761,495

Working Capital Requirements

The meat and processing industry requires a large investment in working capital. Most of the working capital is used to finance the large inventories of slaughter animals. Recent financial records of two firms in the meat industry revealed a net working capital of about 10 percent of sales. Initial working capital requirements would not be quite this large. Total yearly expenses of operations are estimated to be $36,266,839. Assuming that initial working capital requirements are equal to one month's expenses yields a requirement of $3,022,237. This seems to be a reasonable amount considering the methods of payment and factoring services available in the industry.

For purposes of this study, a $3,022,237 investment in working capital was assumed to be the appropriate capital needed to begin operations. This figure is about 8 percent of the anticipated sales revenue. Since the investment in building, land, and equipment totaled $2,761,495, the total capital requirements will be $5,783,732. Thus the proposed venture would be one of the largest undertaken in the state in recent years.

Revenues, Expenses, and ROI

Revenues

The revenue derived from operations will come from two sources: (1) sales of the carcasses of the slaughtered animals, and (2) sales of by-products of the slaughtered operation. As previously pointed out, there will be no processing of hogs into pork products such as bacon, sausage, and the like in the proposed operation. Thus, revenue will come basically from carcass sales and the sales of hides and offal of the slaughtered animals. Output of the plant will be sold primarily to other meat wholesalers and processors. Table B.5 shows the sales revenues from the output of the operation.

Beef sales revenues. The average wholesale price of a beef carcass in 1985 was $67.34 per hundredweight. The estimated average price for hides and offal of cattle was $5.23 per hundred pounds liveweight. Thus, a 900-pound slaughter animal would yield about $364 in carcass sales (5.4 hundredweight [cut] times $67.34), and $47 in hide and offal revenue (9 hundredweight times $5.23).

Total revenue for the 75,000 annual cattle slaughter would amount to $38,503,688—$34,090,875 in carcass revenues and $4,412,813 in revenues from the hides and offal.

Pork sales revenues. The average wholesale value of pork, including by-products, was $43.56 per hundred pounds liveweight in 2005. Since pork is usually processed into bacon, sausage, hams, and the like before being sold to retailers, the wholesale value of pork was used instead of the wholesale price. The difference in the wholesale value and the wholesale price should reflect the additional processing cost or value added by processing.

Pork by-products, including lard, would yield approximately $5.68 per hundredweight. Carcass value would average about $37.85 per hundred-

TABLE B.5. Sales revenues by product type.

Product Type	Number of Hundredweights[a]	Price per lb.[b]	Total Revenue
Beef			
Carcass	506,250	$67.34	$34,090,875
Hides and Offal	843,750	5.23	4,412,813
Total Revenue			$38,503,688
Pork			
Carcass	195,000[c]	$37.85[d]	$7,380,750
Hides and Offal	195,000[e]	5.71[d]	1,113,450
Total Revenue			$8,494,200
Total Revenue—Beef and Pork			$46,997,888

[a]Based on 93,750 cattle and 93,750 hogs slaughtered at an average liveweight of 900 and 208 pounds respectively. Conversion rates of 60 and 70 percent were used in completing the number of hundredweights of each product type.
[b]Based on average prices per hundredweight of carcasses, hides, and offal for 2005.
[c]Dressed weight for cattle and liveweight for hogs.
[d]Estimated from industry revenue percentages for carcasses and by-products.
[e]Liveweight prices for offal and hides are reported in USDA publications in terms of estimates per hundredweight of live animals.

weight. Total revenue from hog slaughter would amount to $8,494,200—$7,380,750 in carcass revenues and $1,113,450 in revenues from by-products.

The combined revenues for the proposed plant would be approximately $46,977,888 in 2005 prices.

Operating Expenses

Four major categories of expenses are discussed in this section: cost of animal inputs, wages and salaries, other employee expenses, and other operating expenses.

Cost of animal inputs. One of the major operating costs for the proposed plant will be the cost of animal inputs. Table B.6 shows the breakdown of these costs. To derive the total cost of each input type, the following basic formula was used:

Total cost of the input = Number of animals
    × (average slaughter weight/one hundred)
    × average price per hundredweight
    + transportation per hundredweight
    × total hundredweights of animals

For the 75,000 cattle supplied through market area sources, a price of $40.53 per hundred weight and a transportation rate of 75¢ was used. A price of $43.15 and a transportation rate of $1.13 was used for the 18,750 cattle to be procured from outside the area. These calculations yielded a total cost of cattle inputs of $35,336,300. This was $27,864,000 for cattle procured in the area and $7,472,300 for animals outside the area.

For hogs, a price of $32 and a transportation rate of 75¢ was used in calculations. This yielded a total cost of hogs inputs of $6,386,300 of the 93,750 annual slaughter. The combined cost of animal inputs totaled $41,722,600.

Wages and salaries. The personnel for the plant totals 127. Of this total, 115 are production or auxiliary personnel with eighty-six of these employees classified as unskilled and twenty-nine as skilled. Information supplied by the USA Employment Security Division allowed an estimate of the industry average wages for jobs classified as unskilled and for skilled workers. Total costs per year for production workers for fifty, forty-hour weeks is $690,375.

The following list shows the office and administrative personnel and yearly salaries for each. Salaries of management personnel quoted are for personnel experienced in the slaughter industry. Total yearly salaries for of-

TABLE B.6. Cost of animal inputs.

Inputs	Number of Animals[a]	Price per 100 lbs.[b]	Total Cost
Cattle within market area	75,000	$41.28	$27,864,000
Cattle outside market area	18,750	44.28	7,472,300
Hogs	93,750	32.75	6,386,300
Totals	$187,500		$41,722,600

[a]Based on the assumption of a 93,750 annual cattle slaughter and 20 percent obtained outside the market area. Average slaughter weights of 900 lbs. and 208 lbs. were used for cattle and hogs respectively.
[b]Prices include transportation costs of 75¢/cwt within the area and $1.13/cwt outside the area.

fice and administrative are $193,500. Total yearly wages and salaries for all personnel are $883,875.

Production manager	$34,250	(includes $1,250 expenses)
Plant manager	38,750	(includes $1,250 expenses)
Production manager	25,000	
Sales manager	21,250	(includes $1,250 expenses)
Personnel manager	15,000	
Receptionist	6,000	
Office workers (6)	38,250	
Accountant	15,000	
Total	$193,500	

Other employee expenses. Other expenses of the proposed operation directly related to personnel are insurance and hospitalization, employment security taxes social security taxes, vacation, holidays, and sick leave, and retirement.

The company's expense for an insurance and hospitalization program would be approximately $26,670. This is based on estimates supplied by a local insurance representative who quoted an industry average of $17.50 per employee. This figure includes average life insurance and hospitalization benefits for the local area. For all plant personnel, monthly premiums would total $2,222.50.

Employment security taxes vary with the claim record of the employer, however, the industry average for the local area is 2.5 percent of total wages and salaries. Assuming a normal employment pattern, the total employment security taxes would be $22,097.

Social security taxes are figured at the rate of 6.85 percent of the first $12,000 in earnings. Using the average wage figures for production and auxiliary personnel, all of the total wages of $690,375 would be subject to social security taxes. Salaries of $119,250 for office and administrative personnel would be subject to social security taxes. Total employer's contribution for social security would be $55,459.

Paid vacation, holidays, and sick leave is figured at ten working days. Total costs would be $27,615. Since salaried personnel are paid on a monthly basis, this figure includes only the additional expenses for wage employees.

A company of this size will have a retirement program for its employees. Because a retirement plan has not been formulated by the originators of the project, the minimal contribution by the employer of such a program is taken as equal to the social security taxes. This is below the industry average: however, it is considered adequate. The following list summarizes the annual expenses for wages, salaries, and employee benefits.

Wages and salaries:
    Production and auxiliary personnel $690,375
    Administrative and office personnel   193,500
Employee benefits:
    Insurance and hospitalization   26,670
    Employment security taxes   22,097
    Social Security taxes   55,459
    Vacation, holidays, and sick leave   27,615
    Retirement   <u>55,459</u>
    Total expenses $1,071,175

Other expenses. In addition to the operation expenses previously estimated, several other categories of expenses should be identified and enumerated.

As was shown earlier, the total investment required in the proposed operation would be about $5,784,250. Assuming all authorized stock is sold and $4,250,000 (value of authorized stock issue minus stock sales commissions and other fees) is available for financing the investment, an additional $1,534,250 would have to be secured through debt financing. The originators of the project plan to apply for an FHA-secured loan for the additional finances needed to begin operations. If this application is accepted, an 8.25 percent loan could be obtained.

Based on a repayment period of twenty-five years and an 8.25 percent interest rate, the debt retirement and interest schedule would be as shown in Table B.7. Total interest charges over the life of the loan would be $1,734,711. This would be an average interest expense of $69,388.

The investment in equipment and building developed earlier was $2,761,995: $1,036,821 for the equipment and $1,725,174 for the building. Assuming the equipment would be depreciated over an eight-year period and the building over a twenty-five-year period, the annual depreciation expense would total $267,490.

The current millage for property taxes in Stevens County is sixty-one mills, and assessed values are about 15 percent of market values. Using this tax rate and structure, the annual property tax for the proposed plant would be $27,668.

The expense for supplies and containers averages about 2.1 percent of total sales. Since there will be no processing of slaughtered animals, a figure of 1 percent of sales was used for the plant. This would be about $469,979 a year. All other expenses are estimated at 3 percent of sales, which is the industry average for regional meat packers. This would be $1,409,937 for the proposed operation on an annual basis. This includes expenses for power, fuel, legal and audit charges, sales expenses, bad debt expense, and so on.

TABLE B.7. Debt retirement and interest schedule.

End of Year	Principal	Interest Charge	Annual Payment
1	$1,534,250	$134,247	$60,970
2	1,463,280	128,037	60,970
3	1,402,310	122,702	60,970
4	1,341,340	117,367	60,970
5	1,280,370	112,032	60,970
6	1,219,400	106,698	60,970
7	1,158,430	101,363	60,970
8	1,077,460	96,028	60,970
9	1,036,490	90,693	60,970
10	975,520	85,358	60,970
11	914,550	80,023	60,970
12	853,580	74,688	60,970
13	772,610	69,353	60,970
14	731,640	64,019	60,970
15	670,670	58,684	60,970
16	607,700	53,349	60,970
17	548,730	48,014	60,970
18	487,760	42,677	60,970
19	426,790	37,344	60,970
20	365,820	32,009	60,970
21	304,850	26,674	60,970
22	243,880	21,340	60,970
23	182,910	16,005	60,970
24	121,940	10,670	60,970
25	60,970	5,335	60,970

Pro Forma Income Statement

Results of the analysis of anticipated revenues and expenses for the proposed venture have been used to develop the pro forma income statement shown in Table B.8. Expenses, including cost of animal inputs, totaled $45,038,237. This amount was subtracted from total sales revenue to deter-

TABLE B.8. Pro forma income statement.

Expense	Cost
Sales	$46,997,888
Cost of inputs	41,722,600
Gross margin	$5,275,288
Expenses	$883,875
Salaries and Wages	
Other employee expenses:	
Insurance	26,670
Retirement	55,459
Vacation and sick leave	27,615
Social Security taxes	55,459
Employment security taxes	22,097
Other Expenses:	
Depreciation	267,490
Interest	69,388
Property taxes	27,668
Supplies	469,979
All other expenses	1,409,937
Total expenses	$3,315,637
Profit before income tax	$1,959,651
Corporate income taxes (federal and state)	$–930,834
Net profit after taxes	$1,028,817

mine profits before taxes. Federal and state corporate income taxes were then subtracted to determine the net profits from operations: $1,028,817.

PV Analysis and ROI

The returns from an investment are defined for decision-making purposes as the net inflows of cash expected from a project. In the case of the proposed venture, this would be equal to the net profit after taxes plus depreciation: $1,296,307. The total capital requirements for the plant were computed to be $5,784,282. The weighted average life of the investment would be eighteen years.

The excess present value is a common technique used to determine whether the returns from an investment justify its capital requirements.

The PV of the returns over the life of the investment are equal to $7,943,769 (51,296,307 × 6.128 at a 15 percent minimum acceptable rate of return). Since the present value of the returns is greater than the capital requirements ($7,943,769 versus $5,784,282) of the project, the proposed venture is economically feasible.

The rate of ROI is computed by dividing net profit after taxes by the total investment. The rate of return for the proposed operation is equal to 17.77 percent.

The rate of return does not consider net cash inflows generated by a project since it is computed using net profits. The net profit figure of $1,028,817 represents only a 2.19 percent return on sales. This return on sales reflects the low overall profitability of the meat industry.

Conclusions

The conclusions reached on the basis of this study are tenable only within the framework of the assumptions made. For example, it was assumed that the level of output would be 187,500 slaughtered animals annually. If, in fact, a higher level of production could be achieved, net profit should be increased. On the other hand, a lower level of output should decrease net profits.

Based on the analysis of the ROI and the PV of the cash flows generated by the investment, the plant is economically feasible. The PV of cash flows over the life of the investment was greater than the investment required to begin operations. Although net profits as a percent of sales are low, the rate of return on investment was estimated at 17.77 percent.

The reader should be cautioned that many of the figures used in this study were estimates based on projections of historical data collected specifically for this study. There is no way to determine the reliability of such estimates; however, these figures are the best estimates available.

Notes

Chapter 1

1. "Ways To Scuttle Your New Business," *Changing Times*, July 1990, pp. 63-65.

Chapter 2

1. See Philip Kotler, *Marketing Management Analysis, Planning, and Control.* Englewood Cliffs, NJ: Prentice Hall, 1980, p. 64.

2. See Derek F. Abell, "Strategic Windows," *Journal of Marketing.* Chicago, IL: July, 1978, pp. 21-26.

3. Ibid., p. 76.

4. See Peter F. Drucker, *Management: Tasks, Responsibilities, Practices.* New York: Harper & Row, 1974, p. 75.

5. Ibid.

6. Colowyo Coal Company, *Colowyo Magazine.* Meeker, CO: Spring 1980, p. 1. Used by permission.

7. Drucker, *Management,* p. 101.

Chapter 4

1. Thompson, Arthur A. and A. J. Strickland. *Strategic Management: Concepts and Cases.* Business Publications, Inc., 1984, p. 152.

2. Porter, Michael E. "How Competitive Forces Shape Strategy," *Harvard Business Review.* 57 #2 (March-April 1979), p. 141.

3. Adapted from McGregor, C. H. and Paul C. Chakmas. *Retail Management Problems,* Fourth Edition. Homewood, IL: Richard D. Irwin, Inc., 1970, pp. 255-256.

4. Alderson, Wroe. *Dynamic Market Behavior.* Homewood, IL: Richard D. Irwin, Inc., 1965, Chapter 8.

5. The section is based on: Kotler, Philip. *Marketing Management: Analysis, Planning, and Control,* Fourth Edition. Englewood Cliffs, NJ: Prentice Hall, Inc., Chapter 11.

Appendix A

1. See Marcia Stepanek, "Weblining," *Business Week E-Biz Supplement*, April 3, 2000, pp. EB26-EB34.

2. See Heather Green, "The Information Gold Mine," *Business Week E-Biz Supplement*, July 26, 1999, pp. EB17-E30.

Index